AN ILLUSTRATED HISTORY OF THE
CIVIL WAR

AN ILLUSTRATED HISTORY OF THE
CIVIL WAR
THE CONFLICT THAT DEFINED THE UNITED STATES

BROOKS D. SIMPSON

SIRIUS

SIRIUS

This edition published in 2021 by Sirius Publishing, a division of
Arcturus Publishing Limited,
26/27 Bickels Yard, 151–153 Bermondsey Street,
London SE1 3HA

ISBN: 978-1-83940-660-7
AD007305US

Printed in China

CONTENTS

Timeline – An Illustrated History of the Civil War

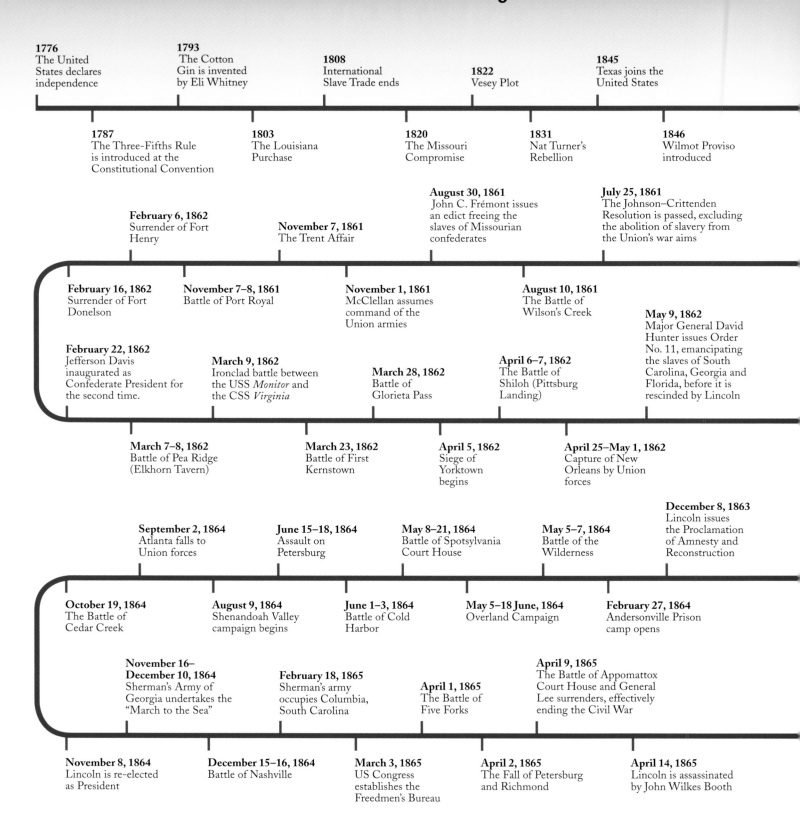

1776
The United States declares independence

1793
The Cotton Gin is invented by Eli Whitney

1808
International Slave Trade ends

1822
Vesey Plot

1845
Texas joins the United States

1787
The Three-Fifths Rule is introduced at the Constitutional Convention

1803
The Louisiana Purchase

1820
The Missouri Compromise

1831
Nat Turner's Rebellion

1846
Wilmot Proviso introduced

August 30, 1861
John C. Frémont issues an edict freeing the slaves of Missourian confederates

July 25, 1861
The Johnson–Crittenden Resolution is passed, excluding the abolition of slavery from the Union's war aims

February 6, 1862
Surrender of Fort Henry

November 7, 1861
The Trent Affair

February 16, 1862
Surrender of Fort Donelson

November 7–8, 1861
Battle of Port Royal

November 1, 1861
McClellan assumes command of the Union armies

August 10, 1861
The Battle of Wilson's Creek

May 9, 1862
Major General David Hunter issues Order No. 11, emancipating the slaves of South Carolina, Georgia and Florida, before it is rescinded by Lincoln

February 22, 1862
Jefferson Davis inaugurated as Confederate President for the second time.

March 9, 1862
Ironclad battle between the USS *Monitor* and the CSS *Virginia*

March 28, 1862
Battle of Glorieta Pass

April 6–7, 1862
The Battle of Shiloh (Pittsburg Landing)

March 7–8, 1862
Battle of Pea Ridge (Elkhorn Tavern)

March 23, 1862
Battle of First Kernstown

April 5, 1862
Siege of Yorktown begins

April 25–May 1, 1862
Capture of New Orleans by Union forces

December 8, 1863
Lincoln issues the Proclamation of Amnesty and Reconstruction

September 2, 1864
Atlanta falls to Union forces

June 15–18, 1864
Assault on Petersburg

May 8–21, 1864
Battle of Spotsylvania Court House

May 5–7, 1864
Battle of the Wilderness

October 19, 1864
The Battle of Cedar Creek

August 9, 1864
Shenandoah Valley campaign begins

June 1–3, 1864
Battle of Cold Harbor

May 5–18 June, 1864
Overland Campaign

February 27, 1864
Andersonville Prison camp opens

November 16–December 10, 1864
Sherman's Army of Georgia undertakes the "March to the Sea"

February 18, 1865
Sherman's army occupies Columbia, South Carolina

April 1, 1865
The Battle of Five Forks

April 9, 1865
The Battle of Appomattox Court House and General Lee surrenders, effectively ending the Civil War

November 8, 1864
Lincoln is re-elected as President

December 15–16, 1864
Battle of Nashville

March 3, 1865
US Congress establishes the Freedmen's Bureau

April 2, 1865
The Fall of Petersburg and Richmond

April 14, 1865
Lincoln is assassinated by John Wilkes Booth

1846–8
The Mexican-American
War

1850
Fugitive Slave Act is
passed as part of the
Compromise of 1850

1851
Uncle Tom's Cabin
is published

1854
The Kansas-Nebraska
Act is passed by Congress

1854–6
"Bleeding Kansas":
Violent conflicts
between abolitionist
and pro-slavery
factions occur

1857
The Dred
Scott Decision

1858
The Lincoln–Douglas
debates

1859
John Brown
leads the
Harpers Ferry
Raid

May 3, 1861
Lincoln calls for volunteers
for the Union Army on a
three-year term

April 17–May 21, 1861
Virginia, Arkansas,
Tennessee, and North
Carolina secede

January–February 1861
Mississippi, Florida, Alabama,
Georgia, Louisiana, and
Texas secede and form the
Confederate States of America

November 6, 1860
Abraham Lincoln
is elected President

July 21, 1861
The Battle of
Bull Run (First
Manassas)

April 19, 1861
Riots take place
in Baltimore

April 12, 1861
Confederate forces
bombard Fort Sumter

December 20, 1860
South Carolina is the
first state to secede

June 25–July 1, 1862
Seven Days' Battles

September 17, 1862
Battle of Antietam
(Sharpsburg)

October 8, 1862
Battle of Perryville
(Chaplin Hills)

December 13, 1862
Battle of
Fredericksburg

May 31–June 1, 1862
The Battle of Seven
Pines (Fair Oaks)

August 30–31, 1862
Battle of Second
Bull Run (Second
Manassas)

October 3–4, 1862
Battle of Corinth

November 7, 1862
Ambrose Burnside
replaces McClellan
as commander of the
Army of the Potomac

**December 31, 1862–
January 3, 1863**
Battle of
Murfreesboro
(Stones River)

September 19–20, 1863
Battle of Chickamauga

July 13–16, 1863
Draft riots in
New York City

May 18–July 4, 1863
The Siege
of Vicksburg

March 3, 1863
The First
Conscription Act

**September–
November, 1863**
The Siege of
Chattanooga

August 21, 1863
Lawrence, Kansas, is
sacked by guerrillas under
the command of William
Clarke Quantrill

July 1–3, 1863
The Battle of
Gettysburg

May 1–4, 1863
The Battle of
Chancellorsville

January 1, 1863
The Emancipation
Proclamation comes
into effect

December 18, 1865
The Thirteenth Amendment
is ratified, ending slavery

July 30, 1866
New Orleans
race riots take
place.

March 4, 1869
Ulysses S. Grant
is inaugurated as
president

March 3, 1877
Rutherford B. Hayes is
inaugurated as President
and ends Reconstruction

April 9, 1866
Civil Rights Act gives
African Americans
equal civil rights

March 1867
The First
Reconstruction
Act is passed

March 30, 1870
Fifteenth Amendment
prohibited using race as a
barrier to voting

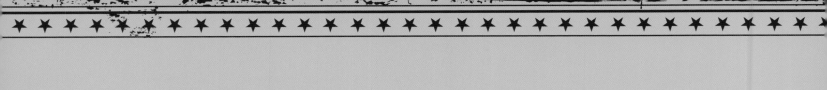

Union Soldiers from the Army of the Potomac in 1862. The Civil War was perhaps the defining moment in American history and it has left a marked impression on the modern psyche.

INTRODUCTION

The American Civil War did much to define what the United States is today and what it hopes to become. The history of the United States is largely the story of how Americans sought to define words such as freedom, liberty, equality, and progress, and the war and its results were fundamental in resolving some disagreements about what those words meant while setting the stage for further discussion and debate. That these conflicts resulted in violent bloodshed to a degree never seen before or since in American history reminds us of the difficulty in resolving those disagreements and the failure of American political institutions to reach satisfactory and lasting compromise settlements. Fate and geography offered them the chance to do so without compromising border security or threatening international conflict that jeopardized the nation-state, yet in the end Americans proved to be the biggest threat to their own continued existence as they battled over the meaning of their experiment in constructing a polity based on principles that often clashed in practice.

This is a concise introduction to the Civil War and Reconstruction era, focusing on the war itself, but also offering brief discussions of how the war came about, how Americans sought to define what the war did (and did not) achieve during Reconstruction, and how memories of the war and debates over its legacy continue down to the present day. It does not pretend to offer comprehensive or indeed in some cases adequate or deserved attention to many topics, as one might expect from the nature of a concise introduction. The literature on the coming of the war and its causes, the conduct of the conflict, and its resolution in war and peace is voluminous and ever-expanding. However, this narrative focuses on politics, policy, and war; it rests upon the assumption that differences over slavery were fundamental to this struggle over American identity and promise, while beliefs about race helped determine its ultimate resolution in what remained an unfinished revolution to realize liberty, equality, and freedom.

Of necessity the narrative paints in broad strokes—introductions are never definitive but offer instead a point of departure for those readers who want to learn more or who sense that something that engages them has been neglected or given short shrift. Yet for those readers coming to the topic with little or no familiarity with this period of American history, the hope is that they will come away from their encounter having gained some basic information and with an appetite to learn more. For how one views the Civil War and Reconstruction remains a key part of how Americans define themselves today, and their understanding of that past is ever changing in light of the demands and challenges of the present. It was no accident that Dr. Martin Luther King, Jr., stood in front of the Lincoln Memorial a century after the issuance of the Emancipation Proclamation to remind Americans to be true to their principles that remained unrealized in practice; and in more recent years Americans have had cause once more to reflect on those principles as they debate what to do about Confederate monuments in light of what they truly represent. It is the author's hope that this slim volume offers readers context with which to explore those issues.

Slaves at work on a plantation in South Carolina, c. 1862. Slavery became the defining feature of Southern society by the outbreak of the Civil War, and led to irreconcilable differences between North and South.

CHAPTER 1
HOW THE WAR CAME

THE CAUSE OF the American Civil War may have best been described by US President Ulysses S. Grant, who declared that it "will have to be attributed to slavery." While he freely admitted that "the great majority of the people of the North had no particular quarrel with slavery," Southern efforts to secure slavery's future at the cost of Northern rights and interests proved too much for white Northerners to bear.

Yet just to say that slavery caused the American Civil War is to simplify the issue beyond recognition. A closer look at how debates over slavery led to the rupture of the American republic offers a clearer understanding of why it did so. Most white Northerners supported going to war in 1861 not in order to free the slaves or to destroy an immoral institution, but to subdue a rebellion that endangered the American experiment in union and republicanism. In turn, the Southern quest for independence was sparked by the feeling among an increasing number of white Southerners that slavery was no longer safe while they remained in that republic, and that only a republic specifically designed to protect the so-called "peculiar institution" of slavery could serve that purpose.

Slavery in American Society

In the eighteenth century slavery was an American institution; white supremacy was a given. The largest concentration of enslaved laborers was in New York City. Nor was slavery necessarily tied to plantation labor: there were many ways for a slaveholder to make money. A convergence of circumstances and events shifted slavery from being a pan-American phenomenon to becoming the cornerstone of Southern society, economic activity, and politics. In several Northern states, the interplay of religious belief and the rhetoric of a revolutionary movement that spoke powerfully about liberty, freedom, equality, and the need to resist enslavement by a corrupt empire chipped away at the institution's foundations, with Pennsylvania and Massachusetts leading the way.

Although slavery was profitable in the North, it was not integral to the social, economic, or political order of the region, so abolition would affect a smaller portion of the white population. The diversification of regional economies north of the Potomac and Ohio rivers opened up new ways to make money that did not rely on the exploitation of enslaved labor. Racism and white supremacy persisted, but many advocates of emancipation had no trouble denouncing slavery as an institution at the same time as retaining their belief that African Americans, enslaved or free, were not the equals of European Americans. Over several decades, support for the eradication of slavery, either immediately or gradually, grew in the Northern states east of the Appalachians and eventually prevailed. To the west, the territories that emerged north of the Ohio, forged out of a Northwest Ordinance that blocked slavery, chose not to make the "peculiar institution" part of their polity when they eventually applied for statehood.

South of the Mason-Dixon line (the state boundary where Pennsylvania and Delaware meet West Virginia and Maryland), changes in plantation agriculture opened up new opportunities to promote slavery's fortunes and ensure its continued profitability. Chief among these was the rise of cotton growing, aided in part by the invention of a means to mechanize the removal of seeds from raw cotton, most famously through the use of Eli Whitney's cotton gin, a machine invented in 1793. Just as the future of tobacco-plantation economies seemed in danger and the use of enslaved labor to grow rice and sugar remained limited to coastal areas, the mechanization of cotton harvesting made its cultivation economically feasible on a

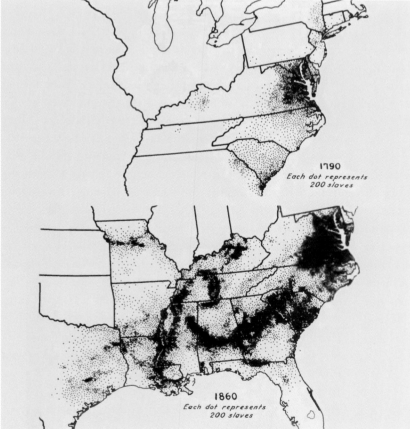

A dot-and-pin map showing the distribution of slavery in the United States in 1790 and 1860.

Eli Whitney's cotton gin, invented in 1793, made cotton-growing significantly more profitable.

large scale beyond coastal areas, where planters found profit in growing finer cotton containing fewer seeds.

By the early decades of the nineteenth century, slavery in the United States had become a distinctively Southern institution. There, forecasts of its ultimate demise had been superseded by claims that it was a vibrant and growing institution. That attitude justified calls for its expansion westward across the cotton frontiers of Georgia, Alabama, Tennessee, and Mississippi, while plantation agriculture in Louisiana also continued to thrive. The growth of textile manufacturing in Great Britain and New England increased the demand for cotton and provided ready markets for its production. With the end of the War of 1812, American overseas trade, especially to Great Britain, stabilized, and territorial expansion westward, involving the spread of the cotton

A slave family on a Smith's plantation in Beaufort, South Carolina, 1862.

dropped or amended lest they promote hostility to slavery. At the Constitutional Convention in 1787, efforts to protect slavery played an integral part in the framing of the US Constitution. The result was a formula (known as the Three-Fifths Rule) whereby an enslaved person would be counted as 60 percent of a free person in determining the allotment of seats in the House of Representatives, votes in the Electoral College that chose the chief executive, and tax burdens. The ensuing document also prevented federal action against the international slave trade for two decades. Without such concessions, the movement to draft the Constitution would have floundered. Slave states thus enjoyed more political power than their free-state counterparts and could defend their interests at the federal level; Virginia dominated control of the executive branch, with but one interruption, until 1825. The Supreme Court, viewed by many Americans as the final arbiter of the meaning of the Constitution, was controlled by pro-slavery jurists, with the two chief justices from 1801 to 1864 hailing from slave states.

The adoption of a new constitution framed in the shadow of a war of independence fueled by egalitarian rhetoric had fundamental implications for the conduct of subsequent debates over policy. Politicians had to prove that their proposals and positions were not only wise, prudent, or necessary, but also constitutional. The very vocabulary of political debate hailed back to Revolutionary rhetoric and constitutional constructs, often guided by a desire to explain what the founders would have done or what they meant. The framework of federalism meant that there would be constant discussion over whether a measure was properly the concern of states or the federal government.

Before long Americans were also arguing over whether the document permitted the possibility

frontier, seemed to guarantee the future of the "peculiar institution." The end of the international slave trade did nothing to dim these expectations, given the growth of its domestic counterpart.

Yet economic innovation can only explain so much. The political defense of slavery mounted by Southerners preceded the introduction of Mr. Whitney's contraption. Delegates from South Carolina and Georgia had expressed their displeasure with Thomas Jefferson's soaring rhetoric in his draft Declaration of Independence when it was presented to the Second Continental Congress in 1775, and demanded that certain phrases be of a state unhappy with the adoption of various measures to block their enforcement or even to consider leaving the Union altogether through a process that became known as secession. Much ink has been spilled on the issue of whether secession was a constitutional right. That debate reflected strong interests as well as political philosophies and logical interpretation born in textual exegesis. Nevertheless, all parties agreed that secession would be undertaken only as a last resort in cases of dire necessity and that it might be resisted by force. However engaging intellectually such matters might be to some people, what energized discussion was a clash of political and economic interests, with an occasional nod to moral beliefs.

Although Americans disagreed over a number of issues, those involving slavery, its protection, and its expansion proved far less susceptible to the grand traditions of bargaining and compromise than did political negotiation in other areas. As plantation slavery prospered, its proponents began to argue for its advantages as a positive good, setting aside earlier claims that it was a necessary evil. Slavery promoted economic opportunity for whites, they said, while providing a system of paternalistic care for the enslaved. Unlike managers and bosses in a free-labor society, who cared little for their workers and could hire or fire them on a whim, leaving those poor souls economically desolate, slave owners took care of their enslaved workers, providing food, shelter,

A mid-19th century painting of the 1787 Constitutional Convention, where the Three-Fifths rule was introduced.

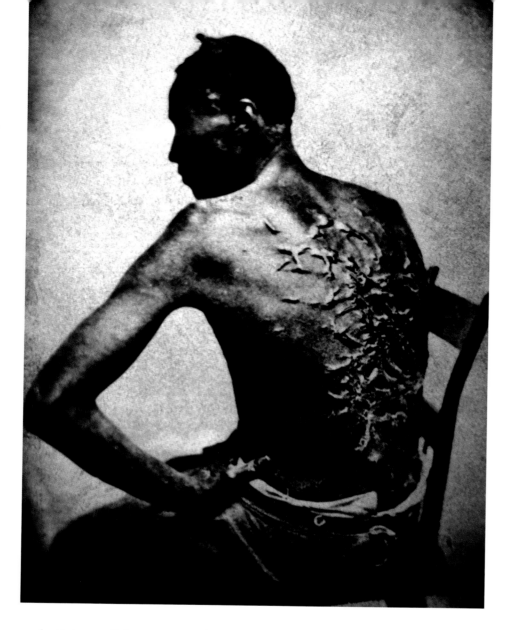

A famous photograph of the scars of Gordon, a slave at a Louisiana plantation. The brutal treatment meted out to slaves belied their masters' claims that slavery was a benevolent institution.

and religious enlightenment—at least so claimed slavery's advocates. Some people went so far as to equate white masters with heads of family, an unfortunate image when it clashed with the reality of the sexual exploitation of enslaved women by whites.

African Americans took umbrage over such justifications of an institution that deprived the enslaved of the freedom, equality, and basic human rights that were the cornerstones of the American experiment in republicanism. They also protested against the broader racism and white supremacy characteristic of American society as a whole which denied African Americans the right to rise and forge their own lives. Racism

and slavery exposed the hypocrisy in American ideals as practiced by white Americans, even as those ideals provided the rhetoric used to attack slavery. Although there were slave rebellions, they were usually unsuccessful, as were efforts to flee plantations that meant leaving loved ones behind. Resistance more often took other forms: slaves used religion and culture to push back against the oppressive and stifling nature of enslavement. Even Southern whites, however much they tried to present slavery as a benevolent institution where slaves smiled, sang, and were content, always worried that one day they would have to confront an insurrection that could engulf their entire world in violence.

MAP OF THE UNITED STATES,

SHOWING BY COLORS

THE AREA OF FREEDOM AND SLAVERY,

AND THE TERRITORIES WHOSE DESTINY IS YET TO BE DECIDED;

EXHIBITING ALSO

THE MISSOURI COMPROMISE LINE

and

THE ROUTES OF COLONEL FREMONT IN HIS FAMOUS EXPLORATIONS.

WITH IMPORTANT STATISTICS OF THE FREE AND SLAVE STATES.

NEW YORK:
PUBLISHED BY G. W. ELLIOTT, 172 WILLIAM STREET.

COMPARISON OF THE CHIEF STATISTICS OF THE FREE STATES AND OF THE SLAVE STATES, ACCORDING TO THE U. S. CENSUS OF 1850.

FREE STATES.

SLAVE STATES.

CONGRESSIONAL REPRESENTATION.

HOUSE OF REPRESENTATIVES.

The Free States have one hundred and forty-four members.

The Slave States have ninety members.

UNITED STATES SENATE

POST-OFFICE STATISTICS FOR A SINGLE YEAR.

AREA OF THE STATES.

PRESIDENTS AND VICE-PRESIDENTS.

SLAVEHOLDERS.

PRESIDENTIAL ELECTORS FOR 1856, AND POPULAR VOTE IN 1852.

The Missouri Compromise

Yet when slaveholding interests pressed for the admission of Missouri as a slave state in 1819, many white Northerners balked. They chafed under the promise of continued Southern domination at the national level, where Southerners (especially Virginians) seemed to exercise unchecked power. The admission of yet another slave state to the Union would increase slavery's sway in national politics. Opponents of slavery's expansion seized upon the notion that the federal government held jurisdiction over the territories and admission to statehood to resist Missouri's bid until they secured several key concessions, including the admission of Maine as a free state (thus maintaining the balance of slave and free states in the Senate) and a promise to restrict the future expansion of slavery into new territories south of Missouri's southern border at 36'30" latitude. The resulting Missouri Compromise (as this offsetting of Maine and Missouri was known), the product in part of the endeavors of the Speaker of the House, Kentuckian Henry Clay, seemed an ideal way to maintain an equilibrium of free and slave states for the time being.

Yet one could not miss the fact that Southern whites, who had once spoken of slavery as a necessary evil that would one day expire (by means not specified), were now promoting its expansion and embracing its political advantages. Northern whites were beginning to wonder about slavery's effects on their own lives. Would Southern political power limit white Northern opportunity or infringe upon Northern rights and interests? Was slavery on the way to ultimate extinction through the operation of inevitable fate, or was it being not only resuscitated, but also robustly revived, with a bright future ahead of it?

The Kentucky Senator Henry Clay was a leading politician and was appointed as Secretary of State in March 1825.

Adding to this concern was the fate of an effort to help facilitate the end of slavery by relocating the emancipated outside the boundaries of the United States, a policy that became known as colonization. What worried some people about the end of slavery was the question of what would happen to the former slaves. Would they become part of the American polity? Would they compete with whites for employment? Would the United States become a multiracial, egalitarian society by choice, much to the fear of whites who firmly believed in the racial inferiority of blacks? The founding of the American Colonization Society at the end of 1816 seemed an ideal answer, especially to people in the upper South, notably Virginia, who were alarmed by the growing numbers of free black people in their midst as well as the potential for a slave insurrection. Emancipation would take place gradually, and the emancipated would leave the United States, preferably returning to the continent from which their ancestors came. After all, a black shipowner from Boston, Paul Cuffee, had already demonstrated that some freed blacks were willing to relocate to Africa, to Sierra Leone. Many prominent political leaders, including Henry Clay, future presidents James Monroe and Andrew Jackson, and Chief Justice John Marshall, supported the idea.

The Abolitionist Movement

But colonization stumbled after securing a foothold in Africa in what would become Liberia. Slaveholders proved unwilling to free their slaves in large numbers, preferring instead that free blacks, rather than slaves, who had long been seen as a disruptive element, were sent away to Africa—a notion which was further reinforced when the freedman Denmark Vesey's plot to hatch a slave insurrection in Charleston, South Carolina, was foiled in 1822. Rather, slavery's defenders became bolder and louder during the 1820s.

Inspired by a wave of religious revivals known as the Second Great Awakening (the first having occurred nearly a century before) calling for the immediate eradication of sin, many whites who had once favored gradual emancipation now demanded immediate abolition. They defined slavery as a sin and sought to convert the sinners (the slaveholders) by convincing them of their error and immorality, offering emancipation of the enslaved as a form of redemption. Chief among this new wave of abolitionists was William Lloyd Garrison, who issued the first number of a new newspaper, *The Liberator*, on January 1, 1831. He declared that immediate abolition was consistent with American political values as expressed in the Declaration of Independence as well as Christian principles, but he did not stop there:

> *I am aware, that many object to the severity of my language; but is there not cause for severity? I will be as harsh as truth, and as uncompromising as justice. On this subject, I do not wish to think, or speak, or write, with moderation. No! No! ... I am in earnest—I will not equivocate—I will not excuse—I will not retreat a single inch— AND I WILL BE HEARD.*

A certificate from the American Colonization Society. The society hoped to send free African Americans to West Africa, partly to assuage white fears.

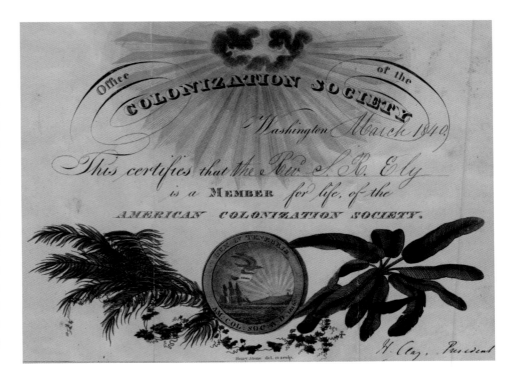

The Nat Turner Rebellion of 1831 was a dramatic and terrifying example of organized slave resistance. Many Southerners believed that the abolitionist message had encouraged the rebellion.

Although Garrison and his followers would claim they were using "moral suasion" to persuade slaveholders to see the error of their ways, white Southerners saw something else—namely a new way to castigate white Southerners while sparking insurrection. For decades to come, Garrison and other immediate abolitionists would not find favor with many Northerners either. In fact, they were targeted by mobs, including one which murdered abolitionist minister and newspaper editor Elijah Lovejoy in Alton, Illinois, in 1837. White Southerners, angry at being denounced as immoral and petrified by the potential for insurrection (made manifest in Southampton County, Virginia, when the enslaved preacher Nat Turner led a bloody uprising that killed approximately 60 white men, women, and children in August 1831), moved quickly to stifle the abolitionist message and prevent it from being transmitted southward. It was in Southerners' reaction to the abolitionist message that the escalation of the debate over slavery began in earnest.

At the same time, white Southerners devised a more coherent articulation of the principle of secession that previous thinkers had only glimpsed, notably in the Virginia and Kentucky Resolutions of 1798. Those documents had offered ways for states to oppose and interdict what they believed to be transgressions of the constitutional compact by the national authority, although they left unanswered what might happen should such oppression continue. South Carolina's John C. Calhoun, President Andrew Jackson's former vice president and once a fervent nationalist, now devoted his considerable intellectual powers to devising a theory of nullification that would serve the same purpose of checking national power, but slowly he began to expand beyond that to outline remedies should initial resistance fail to deter. In the wake of Chief Justice John Marshall's efforts to establish the Supreme Court as the ultimate arbiter of constitutional interpretation, Calhoun insisted that as the Constitution was a contract between the states (an assumption challenged by others, notably Daniel Webster of Massachusetts), it was left to the contracting agents to determine the terms and meaning of the contract as well as whether it had been violated. If a contracting party determined that the violations breached the contract, then it could choose to leave.

Calhoun ostensibly developed his theory of interposition and nullification in response to federal tariff legislation, which he viewed as harmful to Southern plantation interests that relied upon an export economy, but the inference was clear: should the federal government take measures harmful to slavery, slaveholding states might exercise the option to leave the Union. When Calhoun and his followers sought to implement his theory by nullifying tariff legislation, however, President Jackson threatened military action against South Carolina. Henry Clay, who had just lost a bid to unseat Jackson in the presidential election of 1832, quickly engineered a compromise whereby all parties could claim victory in the wake of lower tariff rates, but Calhoun's principle remained intact, at least in the minds of secessionists. The more frequently the threat of secession was invoked, the more it looked like political blackmail.

Resistance to the circulation of the abolitionist message created a new flashpoint of conflict in the mid-1830s. Invoking the right of petition, men and women showered their representatives in Washington with requests that Congress take various actions adverse to slavery. Southern representatives moved to have such petitions suspended without reading them, silencing the threat through the so-called Gag Rule. Northern representatives, led by former president John Quincy Adams, sought to challenge the rule at every opportunity. People who cared little about the abolition of slavery nevertheless deplored the willingness of Southerners to compromise the political rights of Northerners to engage in political debate. Similarly, Southerners sought to bar the circulation of abolitionist literature through the federal mail system, claiming that it incited insurrections and violence.

Dramatic as the confrontations appeared to be, they were usually not the dominant issues debated in American politics during the 1830s and into the 1840s. Rather, economic policy, whether it be a federal bank or banking as a whole, tariff policy, or federal support for internal improvements, dominated discussion, while federal policy toward indigenous Americans and foreign policy also sparked interest. The two major political parties, the Whigs and Democrats, clashed over these issues, while internal sectional divisions within each party surfaced when the issue of slavery appeared in one of its many manifestations. Efforts at establishing an avowedly abolitionist or antislavery party proved unsuccessful at

John C. Calhoun helped develop the legal framework for secession, arguing that the Union was a contract, and if the federal government broke its terms, then the states would be free to leave.

General Winfield Scott enters Mexico City in 1847. The Mexican–American War (1846–8) proved a training ground for many of the officers who fought in the Civil War.

drawing more than a sliver of voters. However, a pattern was beginning to emerge whereby white Southerners, acting on slavery's behalf, adopted measures that seemed excessive to a growing number of white Northerners who, regardless of how they felt about slavery, saw their own rights, liberties, and interests at stake.

The debate over slavery became more visible in the 1840s. Once more, territorial expansion was to blame. Having won independence from Mexico in 1836, the Republic of Texas, headed by white slaveholding Southerners, sought to join the United States. Opponents resisted slavery's expansion and increase in political power yet again, but Texas became part of the United States in 1845. However, there remained a dispute as to the location of the border between Texas and Mexico, and in that debate lay the seeds of yet another war, this time stripping away a significant chunk of northern Mexico stretching all the way to the Pacific Ocean—lands slaveholders claimed to covet, although plantation agriculture would have to give way to other uses of enslaved labor. Northerners, already angry that the presidential administration of James K. Polk had slighted Northern economic interests by rejecting a measure to spend federal funds to improve rivers and harbors, could not abide fighting a war and absorbing yet more territory earmarked for slavery. Pennsylvania congressman David Wilmot offered a rider to a military appropriations bill that said that none of the money to be spent could be used to acquire territory where slavery would be allowed.

What soon became known as the Wilmot Proviso never passed both houses of Congress, but it demonstrated how slavery could split both parties sectionally—especially as Wilmot, a Democrat, was opposing the head of his own party, the Tennessean Polk. Moreover, Wilmot's grievance was in part a response to Southerners using their political power to thwart Northern economic development, and how that power was buttressed by the continued expansion of slavery.

By decade's end, a series of issues, all related to slavery, threatened national unity. Some people deplored the existence of the slave trade in the District of Columbia within sight of the Capitol building; others protested against efforts to interfere with the return of fugitive slaves as provided for in the Constitution. The discovery of gold in California pushed the question of its statehood to the forefront of the political agenda, while Texans now feuded with New Mexicans over where one state ended and the other began.

TOWN & COUNTRY MAKING ANOTHER DRIVE AT THE GREAT QUESTION.—NO GO!!

The Compromise of 1850

An aging Henry Clay attempted to wrap all these issues up in a single bill that had something for everyone, but this time the spirit of compromise failed. News came that representatives from several Southern states would convene in Nashville to consider their options should nothing happen. In his last major speech on the Senate floor, John C. Calhoun threatened secession if the South did not get its way; New York senator William Henry Seward spoke of a higher law than the Constitution that justified resistance to slavery;

Daniel Webster supported Clay's endeavors and called for compromise. It was left to Illinois senator Stephen A. Douglas, a Democrat, to unravel the impasse by taking apart Clay's bill and passing each component measure supported by shifting majorities, allowing everyone to claim that they had not sold out their section. Thus the Compromise of 1850 was enacted.

The most problematic component of the Compromise was the revised Fugitive Slave Act, intended to beef up previous flawed legislation. A commissioner appointed by the federal government would determine whether the alleged fugitive slave brought before him was in fact a fugitive slave—and would be compensated twice as much per case if he returned the alleged fugitive to slavery. This process set aside a jury trial in favor of a system of compensation that invited fraud. Federal marshals could also require local citizens to assist in the recovery of fugitive slaves by mobilizing a posse, forcing people who wanted nothing to do with slavery to enforce federal law—note that white Southerners were not shy about

A political cartoon from the 1848 Presidential election, in which the Wilmot Proviso proved a key issue.

using federal power so long as it was to support slavery. Nonetheless, some Northerners resisted the enforcement of the act and assisted in the escape of several fugitives, causing Southerners to wonder whether slavery was still safe within the Union. Southerners also grew uneasy when Harriet Beecher Stowe's serialized novel *Uncle Tom's Cabin* appeared, starting in 1851. Its heart-rending portrayal of slavery's evils, especially in breaking up families, moved many readers, and added to the moral castigation of the South.

The political environment also shifted in the years following the Compromise of 1850. Democrats struggled to contain sectional rifts within their party by rallying the partisan faithful to battle their Whig foes. But the Whig party was on its last legs: its leaders, notably Clay and Webster, passed from the scene, while the party's distinctive stand on using government to nurture economic development lost its luster as prosperity rendered such aid unnecessary and Democrats dropped their doctrinaire opposition to proposals requiring government assistance. When Whigs wavered in their skepticism concerning Catholicism and immigration in the wake of a surge of immigrants, mostly from Ireland and Germany, during the past decade, voters suspicious of the new arrivals cast aside the Whigs to express their concerns through the newly-founded nativist Know Nothing Party. Without Whig foes, Democrats no longer needed to embrace the necessity of party unity with such fervent desire, and before long divisions along sectional lines—in other words, based on narrower, localized issues—appeared.

Slaves are returned to their masters under the provisions of the 1850 Fugitive Slave Act.

Bleeding Kansas

Sectional politics was sparked in earnest by Stephen Douglas's pet project to provide for a transcontinental railroad with its eastern terminus favoring his home state of Illinois. To achieve that end, he advocated the organization of two new territories, Kansas and Nebraska, just west of Missouri. A group of Southern Democratic senators, known as the F Street Mess for their practice of dining together at the same establishment, blocked the project, insisting that the price for their support would be Douglas's explicit repudiation of the Missouri Compromise's prohibition of slavery's expansion in lands that included the proposed territories. Douglas readily agreed, adopting instead the philosophy of popular sovereignty, which called for the people who settled in a territory to determine whether it would welcome slavery. This deceptively simple solution at first glance promised to remove debates about slavery's expansion from the national stage, but its vagueness left open questions about when such a determination would be made during the course of territorial development. Could the initial group of settlers who hurried out to the territory in question determine that territory's fate for subsequent waves of migrants? Would Northerners readily accept the end of a time-honored political compromise that had fallen casualty to what was becoming increasingly known as the "slave power," namely white Southerners who would do whatever was necessary to promote the interests of slavery? Would such actions continue to come at the expenses of the rights, liberties, and opportunities cherished by white Northerners?

Although the Kansas-Nebraska Act passed Congress in 1854, opposition to the measure soon found more formal expression in the formation of the Republican Party. The new partisan organization drew support across the North from disaffected Democrats and Whig refugees as well as naturally antislavery politicians and voters. It targeted its Democratic counterparts in the North as beholden to their Southern slaveholding

A confrontation between abolitionists and "border ruffians" at Fort Scott, Kansas.

The caning of Massachusetts senator Charles Sumner in Congress, 1856.

compatriots while it vied with Know Nothing efforts to attract anti-Democratic support. By limiting its position to opposing slavery's expansion, it attracted a broader base of support than had it depended upon endorsement of abolition or opposition to slavery itself. The party scored initial successes in the 1854 congressional elections and prepared to put forth a presidential candidate in 1856, while developing a leadership cadre of former Whigs William Henry Seward of New York and Abraham Lincoln of Illinois as well as former Democrats, including Salmon P. Chase of Ohio and the Blair family of Maryland and Missouri.

Meanwhile the efforts to establish a territorial government in Kansas turned violent. Pro-slavery forces from Missouri earned their name as "border ruffians" by jumping across the Missouri state line armed and ready to fight. In response, antislavery forces also armed themselves, and the two sides repeatedly clashed in an effort to secure control of what soon became known as "Bleeding Kansas." Violence spread to the floor of Congress as well in May 1856 in the aftermath of a pro-slavery attack at Lawrence, Kansas, which sparked a lengthy, personal, and biting address by Massachusetts

senator Charles Sumner. Angered by Sumner's improperly personal references to South Carolina senator Andrew Butler, who was absent when Sumner launched his philippic, Butler's kinsman Preston Brooks sought Sumner out at the close of business one afternoon and beat him senseless with a cane, adding "Bleeding Sumner" to "Bleeding Kansas" as evidence of the violent nature of Southern aggression.

Once more white Southerners had crossed the line in defending slavery, at least in the eyes of those voters who believed that it was time to put a stop to the machinations of the so-called slave-power conspiracy by voting Republican. In the fall, presidential race Republican candidate John Charles Frémont, renowned for his exploits in exploring the West, carried a majority of the Northern states but fell short of besting Democratic rival James Buchanan for the presidency, with the Know Nothing candidate, former president Millard Fillmore, finishing a poor third (with most of his support coming from the South). If the Republicans could build on their gains by securing majorities in Buchanan's home state of Pennsylvania and either Indiana or Illinois, they would be able to lay claim to the White House four years hence.

The Dred Scott Decision and the Lincoln–Douglas Debates

In March 1857 the United States Supreme Court, an institution dominated by Southern-born judges, added even more fuel to the fire when it ruled that Dred Scott of Missouri, despite having resided in a free territory as well as a free state, was, with his wife Harriet, still considered a slave. Chief Justice Roger B. Taney of Maryland, rejecting the safety of a narrowly based decision, proclaimed that all black men, not just those who were enslaved, enjoyed no rights that white men "were bound to respect." He added that congressional efforts to curtail the expansion of slavery into the territories or to delegate that authority to territorial governments were an unconstitutional deprivation of slaveholders' property rights. For the moment, it seemed that only when applying for statehood could a territory make the determination whether to bar slavery, but in Taney's opinion lay the seeds of a claim that any prohibition of slavery, even at the state level, was an unjust deprivation of the right to own slaves. The opinion appeared to validate the Republican charge that pro-slavery forces recognized no barriers, while Douglas had to devise a way to salvage the principle of popular sovereignty in light of the majority opinion's crippling blow against his argument that the best way to contain slavery's expansion was at the territorial stage.

Within months a serious collapse in American financial markets, christened the Panic of 1857, dealt a particularly devastating blow to the Northern economy, sparking Southern celebrations of the superiority of a slave-based plantation economy that prospered while providing for its black workers and elevating white opportunity. In contrast, declared one South Carolina senator, Northern white workers were the "mudsills" of society, struggling through unemployment and poverty. Once more Southern Democrats resisted passing legislation to provide indirect economic relief through federal expenditures and adjusted tariff rates. Northern Democrats found themselves under attack by Republicans as subverting Northern opportunity.

The Panic of 1857 threatened Northern economic supremacy. News of the downturn spread rapidly through the country due to the telegraph, leading to a run on the banks.

Dred Scott, a slave from Missouri, argued that he should be considered free as he had lived in Illinois, a free state, for four years.

In Illinois, Republicans nominated Abraham Lincoln to contest Douglas's bid for re-election to the Senate. The lanky former Whig blasted his opponent for failing to defend Northern white interests while insisting on the fundamentally moral nature of the slavery issue. Desperate to save what was left of popular sovereignty, Douglas declared that local voters could effectively nullify the impact of the Dred Scott decision by failing to pass legislation essential to the protection of slavery, leaving it vulnerable—a position that led Southern Democrats to desert him as a possible presidential candidate for 1860. Douglas's claims that Lincoln's opposition to slavery masked a commitment to racial equality, a claim Lincoln denied, proved more effective in securing his eventual re-election,

but the damage to his national political aspirations would not be undone.

In 1850 in Nashville, Tennessee, white Southerners had whispered that they might consider secession if they did not get their way; in 1856 there was open talk of secession should the Republicans prevail in the presidential contest that year. In 1859, the violent actions of an extreme abolitionist petrified white Southerners. John Brown, who resembled a fiery Old Testament prophet, had garnered national attention in 1856 when he led a group of men on a murderous rampage against pro-slavery families in Kansas in retaliation for the attack on Lawrence. Yet several prominent antislavery Northerners still entertained Brown's notion of a raid to promote

The debates between Abraham Lincoln (left) and Stephen Douglas (right) in 1858 drew large crowds and helped Lincoln attain national prominence.

a slave rebellion by freeing and arming slaves who would then establish a rallying point for fellow slaves seeking freedom. Arguing that the political system had failed to devise a way to end slavery peacefully, Brown advocated a violent overthrow of the system, beginning with the seizure of the federal armory at Harpers Ferry, Virginia. At best Brown's plan seemed improbable, but a series of mistakes guaranteed disaster, as first local and then federal forces trapped Brown and compelled his surrender. Facing a death sentence for committing treason against Virginia, Brown turned his trial into an indictment of slavery and the American inability to end it, in the process transforming himself into a martyr for the abolitionist cause. Just as the fact that in 1856 many white Southerners had cheered Preston Brooks for clubbing Sumner angered white Northerners, that a good number of Northerners actually celebrated Brown's exploits shocked white Southerners, who increasingly came to believe that slavery was unsafe so long as the South remained in the Union.

John Brown's raid on Harpers Ferry in 1859 sought to end slavery by promoting rebellions across the South.

Election and Secession

The American political system as a process of compromise collapsed in 1860. Southern Democrats, rejecting Douglas's bid for the presidency, broke away from the party and nominated their own candidate, Vice President John C. Breckinridge of Kentucky. Conservative unionists of various political lineages backed the candidacy of Tennessee's John Bell, while Republicans, sensing victory, set aside the claims of preconvention favorite William Henry Seward of New York, who had made his fair share of enemies while speaking of an "irrepressible conflict," in favor of the Illinoisan Lincoln, whose assertion that "a house divided against itself cannot stand" was scarcely less radical but was lesser known. In the fall contest, Lincoln won the popular vote and was able to translate this into an Electoral College majority due to his strength in the more populous North, and claimed the White House.

A map of the Presidential Election of 1860, showing the breakdown of votes for the four candidates in the various states.

PRESIDENTIAL ELECTION OF 1860

SCALE OF MILES
0   50   100   200   300   400

Lincoln   Breckenridge   Bell   Douglas

Circles show next highest vote for each candidate as above.
Numbers show vote cast for highest and next highest.
Numbers in brackets (6) show electoral vote of state.
Electoral vote of New Jersey was divided: 4 for Lincoln, 3 for Douglas.
Breckenridge received 44.7 per cent of the Southern vote, and Bell received 40.4 per cent.

TERRITORY LEFT UNORGANIZED 1859

62,811
26,693
MAINE (8)

22,069
11,920
MINNESOTA (4)

MICHIGAN

Lake Superior

86,110
65,021
WISCONSIN (5)

88,480
65,047
(6)

NH 6849 33808
VT 25881 5870 (5)

MASSACHUSETTS Lincoln 106,533 Douglas 34,372

NEW YORK
362,616
312,510
(35)

RHODE ISLAND Lincoln 12,244 Douglas 13,701

CONNECTICUT Lincoln 43,882 Douglas 15,522

70,409
55,111
I O W A (1)

172,161
160,215
ILLINOIS (11)

139,033
115,509
INDIANA (13)

231,610
187,232
O H I O (23)

268,030
178,871
PENNSYLVANIA (27)

58324 (4) NEW JERSEY 62801 (3)

42482 41760 MD. (8)

DELAWARE Breckenridge 7,347 Bell 3,864

58,801
58,372
MISSOURI (9)

66,058
53,143
KENTUCKY (12)

74,681
74,323
VIRGINIA (15)

APPALACHIAN MTS.

28,732
20,094
ARKANSAS (4)

INDIAN TERRITORY

69,274
40,797
(4)

64,709
TENNESSEE (12)

48,339
(10)
NORTH CAROLINA
44,990

47,548
15,438
T E X A S (4)

Rio Grande

20,204
LOUISIANA
22,681
(3)

25,040
MISS. (7)

48,831
27,825
ALABAMA (9)

51,889
42,886
GEORGIA (10)

SO. CAROLINA Electors chosen by legislature (8)

8543
5437
FLORIDA (3)

ATLANTIC

O C E A N

GULF OF MEXICO

BAHAMA ISLANDS

BORMAY ENG. CO., N.Y.

In the wake of Lincoln's election, secessionist supporters in the Deep South decided not to wait until the Republicans took office. Starting in South Carolina on December 20, 1860, they seized upon the "lame duck" period to declare that they had left the Union. The debates over secession and the various declarations offered in its justification evidenced that the future of slavery was at the center of deliberations: even most opponents of secession argued that it was a valid measure whose time had not yet come and which might spark a conflict that would endanger slavery. By the following February, seven seceded states had formed the Confederate States of America, an explicitly pro-slavery republic, with its own constitution, congress, and provisional president, Jefferson Davis of Mississippi, along with a call for 100,000 men to enter military service for a year. Secessionists and Confederates seized US installations and gathered US ordnance in preparation for a confrontation.

Desperate efforts in Washington to construct one final compromise floundered when president-elect Lincoln refused to offer concessions on the expansion of slavery; the only measure that emerged was a proposed constitutional amendment that prohibited Congress from abolishing slavery. Secessionists were not fooled: what the Republicans might be forbidden from doing directly did not prevent them from taking other measures that would impair slavery's present and endanger its future. Meanwhile, eight other states where slavery remained a viable concern waited to see what would happen next before deciding whether to join their departed brethren.

Lincoln took the oath of office on March 4 determined to resist secession, but remained open to negotiation. Circumstances forced a rapid resolution of the stalemate when it was learned that the US forces garrisoning Fort Sumter in Charleston Harbor, South Carolina, had six weeks of provisions on hand. To abandon Sumter would be to hand the Confederates a symbolic victory, but it might buy some badly needed time to negotiate, especially if the slave states still in the Union would stand back. After a while, however, Lincoln came to doubt that he would profit by concession, and eventually he decided to resupply the garrison to maintain his authority. This Davis and the Confederates could not accept. When the garrison's commander refused to surrender, the Confederates bombarded the fort on April 12, 1861. The garrison capitulated; Lincoln called for volunteers to put down a rebellion; and four slaveholding states (Virginia, North Carolina, Tennessee, and Arkansas) decided to cast their lot with the Confederacy, while Kentuckians sought protection under the notion that they could remain neutral. Thus the war came.

The inauguration of Jefferson Davis at Montgomery, Alabama on February 18, 1861.

Secession Hall in Charleston, South Carolina. Formerly known as St. Andrew's Hall, it was here that the delegates of the state voted 169 to 0 in favor of secession.

The bombardment of Fort Sumter on April 12, 1861, marked the opening salvo of the Civil War.

CHAPTER 2
CALL TO ARMS

THROUGHOUT THE SPRING of 1861, both the United States and the Confederacy prepared for war. Anticipating the possibility of armed conflict, the Confederates made good use of the materiel they had secured in seizing arsenals and armories throughout the South. Meanwhile, four new states were absorbed: Virginia, North Carolina, Tennessee, and Arkansas, making for a total of 11 Confederate states. The new arrivals augmented the insurrectionary republic's manpower, resources, and territory. Virginia in particular proved valuable. Not only did it bring with it the Tredegar Iron Works in Richmond, but it also meant that several key military leaders would cast their lot with the Confederacy, most notably Robert E. Lee, whose military reputation was known to the political leadership of both sides. In recognition of Virginia's importance, Confederate authorities decided to relocate the national capital from Montgomery, Alabama, to Richmond, a scant 100 miles south of Washington. Nevertheless, in western Virginia, western North

Carolina, and the eastern portion of Tennessee—areas dominated by the Appalachian Mountains—opposition to secession was visible if not successful.

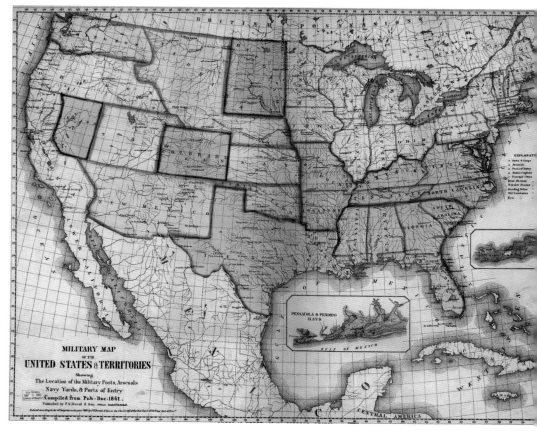

MILITARY MAP
OF THE
UNITED STATES & TERRITORIES
Showing
The Location of the Military Posts, Arsenals
Navy Yards, & Ports of Entry
Compiled from Pub - Dec - 1861.
Published by P. S. Duval & Son.

A map showing the division between seceding states (blue), border states (red), and free states (orange).

Like the remaining United Sates, the Confederacy was never quite as united as its founders desired.

For the United States, the loss of more states posed new challenges. With Virginia's departure, Washington was now vulnerable to Confederate incursions northward across the Potomac River. Meanwhile, four other slave states also contemplated secession. Although Delaware never seriously considered joining the Confederacy, there was substantial support for secession in parts of Maryland, Kentucky, and Missouri. The loss of these three states could prove crippling to the Union cause. If Maryland joined the Confederacy, Washington would be surrounded by Confederate territory. Should Kentucky join, the Ohio River would offer a defensive perimeter to fend off Union invasions and the Confederates could deprive the Union of a major commercial waterway. Finally, if Missouri sided with the Confederacy, the loss of St. Louis and the ability to interfere with commerce along the Mississippi would also compromise Northern commerce.

Lincoln moved quickly to secure Maryland for the United States after secessionist mobs interfered with the transfer of Union infantry regiments southward, including an attack on the 6th Massachusetts Infantry while it was changing trains at Baltimore. The president authorized the suspension of the privilege of the writ of habeas corpus, allowing United States authorities to arrest and hold without trial individuals suspected of aiding the secessionist forces. One of those arrested, John Merryman, sought to challenge his

The 6th Massachusetts Infantry fights on the streets of Baltimore, April 19, 1861.

at least for the moment: secessionist sentiment was strongest in the eastern part of the state, including Baltimore, but to the west allegiance to the Union remained high.

In Missouri the state's governor also contemplated supporting secession, but a United States captain named Nathaniel Lyon moved quickly (some would say hastily or recklessly) to seize the federal arsenal in St. Louis, followed by the capture of elements of the state militia which might be used to support the governor's effort to secure secession by force of arms. Although secessionist sentiment pervaded in parts of Missouri, Lyon had saved St. Louis for the Union. In contrast, both sides were far more cautious in their approach to Kentucky's ultimate allegiance following that state's decision to declare itself neutral, thus closing off the state to both sides. Realizing Kentucky's strategic importance in securing control of the Ohio River, Lincoln did not press the matter. It would not be until late summer that the situation in all three states would become clearer.

The Balance Sheet

By the late spring, it was easier to assess the strengths and weaknesses of both sides. The Union had far more population to draw on than did the Confederacy, with some 23 million people, only a small number of whom were enslaved, opposing some nine million in Confederate territory, nearly 40 percent of whom were enslaved. Both sides had to build their military forces almost from scratch: the peacetime United States army in 1860 numbered some 16,000 men, with several high-ranking officers declaring allegiance to the Confederacy. Nor did either side have much in terms of naval forces, let alone vessels prepared to wage war along the rivers as well as the seacoast. To be sure, the Union forces could draw upon far superior manufacturing and transportation resources: for every factory worker in the Confederacy there was a factory in Union territory, and most of the United States' industrial output (as well as a majority of its foodstuffs) had come from the North.

Captain Nathaniel Lyon took control of the federal arsenal at St. Louis, Missouri, and kept the state in the Union despite the secessionist tendencies of Governor Claiborne Jackson.

arrest: when Union authorities failed to deliver Merryman for a hearing, Chief Justice Roger B. Taney, asking in his capacity as a federal circuit court judge, denounced Lincoln's suspension of the writ as unconstitutional, claiming that such an act was reserved to Congress. Lincoln ignored the ruling, later claiming that the national emergency he faced required prompt action. The Maryland legislature declined to advocate secession, while Union military authorities placed Baltimore under martial law. Maryland would remain in the Union,

COTTON IS KING!

Old England is mighty; Old England is free;
She boasts that she ruleth the waves of the sea;
(But between you and I, that's all fiddle-de-dee;)
She cannot, O Cotton! she cannot rule thee.
Lo! Manchester's lordling thy greatness shall own,
And yield more to thee than he would to the Throne:
For before thee shall bend his fat marrow-bone,
And deaf be his ear to the live chattel's groan.

However, victory would not be easy for the Union. The Confederacy was on the defensive; and Union victory was defined in terms of the destruction of the Confederacy, which meant regaining control of some 750,000 square miles, an area rivaling that of Napoleon's empire. Moreover, the Confederacy's chief export, cotton, was highly valued in Great Britain and (to a lesser extent) France, giving the newly founded slaveholding republic some leverage in foreign affairs and inspiring thoughts of European arbitration or intervention that would lead to a recognition of Confederate independence. Thus, even as Lincoln declared a blockade of Confederate-controlled ports in order to deny the enemy the opportunity to import arms and supplies from abroad, the Confederacy, proclaiming that King Cotton would eventually prevail, urged plantation owners not to export cotton in order to bring Europe to its knees, and thereby forcing European nations to intervene on the side of the Southerners. This proved a somewhat problematic strategy at first, for booming cotton production during the previous years meant that European warehouses were already filled to capacity. It would take some time for the effects of a cotton embargo to be felt.

The Fate of Slavery

Confederate strength rested in part upon the utilization of enslaved labor as a primary means of production as well as the foundation of white Southern society. Slave labor allowed the Confederacy to mobilize a far higher percentage of its white adult male population for military service without dipping into the labor force. Enslaved workers and servants could also accompany Confederate armies in the field, performing tasks such as food preparation, staffing transportation services, and digging fortifications, thus freeing Confederate soldiers for combat duty.

Yet the institution of slavery also challenged the Confederate war effort. It would be difficult to concede hard-to-defend terrain to Union forces if that meant leaving plantations vulnerable, but shifting slaves to defended areas would be an arduous task. For all the talk of the loyalty of enslaved workers, there was always the whispered threat of rebellion. Moreover, should Confederate military authorities assume control of slaves for military purposes, slaveholders might ponder whether their right to own private property might be compromised to wage a war intended to preserve that very right.

For the United States, to attack slavery directly came at a political cost. Those Democrats who supported a war to reunite the republic might well balk if that war was now being waged to free the slaves. Furthermore, given that Lincoln's objective was to reunite the nation, targeting slavery would only complicate that task by alienating white Southerners who pledged to fight to the bitter end to preserve the "peculiar institution." Yet to keep one's hands off slavery was to leave untouched one of the primary advantages the Confederacy enjoyed in fighting for its independence. Unless the Union could win a war while operating under such constraints, it might have to accept the necessity of an escalation that embraced emancipation. Nevertheless, in July 1861 Congress passed a joint resolution declaring that the United States would not make any changes to slavery, a notion that met with the approval of its slave-state sponsors, Kentucky representative John J. Crittenden and Tennessee senator Andrew Johnson.

By the time Johnson and Crittenden acted, however, it was already too late. Abstract notions of fighting a war that did not affect slavery quickly gave way in the face of reality. As United States military forces began advancing across Confederate territory, they disrupted slavery. The proximity of enemy military forces offered slaves a chance to escape to safety. Three slaves did so in May 1861, presenting themselves before Union major general Benjamin F. Butler at Fort Monroe, Virginia. Learning that the three fugitives had been working on Confederate fortifications, Butler rejected demands that they be returned to Confederate lines, arguing that as slaves were considered property by the Confederates and that they were being used for military purposes, they could be captured and held on the grounds that

they were contraband of war. The decision did not free any slaves: it simply transferred ownership to the United States of America. In August the very Congress that weeks earlier had declared that the war had nothing to do with slavery endorsed Butler's interpretation when it passed what later became known as the First Confiscation Act, holding that slaves being used for military purposes by Confederate authorities were subject to capture and confiscation.

Beyond this President Lincoln would not go. To move against slavery at a time when it was yet an open question as to the ultimate allegiance of Maryland, Kentucky, and Missouri would be to risk tipping the scales in favor of secession in those slave states. Thus when, at the end of August, Major General John C. Frémont, who had been the Republican Party's first candidate for president in 1856, decided to impose martial law in Missouri and declared free all slaves owned by secessionist masters in the state, the president, aware that Kentucky's neutrality lay in the balance, rescinded the order after Frémont refused to withdraw it. Lincoln believed there was no need to spark trouble where none existed. For the moment it might be easier to entice white

Slaves built the Confederate Fort in Charleston, South Carolina, in 1863. The South was not averse to using slaves in a supporting role in their military endeavors.

Major General Irvin McDowell was placed in command of the Army of Northern Virginia, but his skills lay in logistics and organization rather than on the front lines.

Southerners to return to the Union voluntarily if they believed that slavery would remain as it was than to arouse a more bitter confrontation that would cost the administration some of the support it so desperately needed to wage war successfully.

At the beginning of the war Lincoln could only call upon states to provide volunteers for 90 days; that initial term of service would expire during the second half of July. Although subsequent calls to raise troops requested two and then three years of service, the 90-day boys would have to do for the time being. The news that the Confederate Congress would convene at Richmond on July 20 increased the pressure on Lincoln to do something. He continued to press Major General Irvin McDowell, who had taken charge of the streams of recruits and regiments that had come to Washington, to advance into Virginia. McDowell, realizing his men were still inexperienced, even raw, sought time to train them, but the president, like most Northerners, was eager for action. "You are green, it is true," he told McDowell; "but they are green, also; you are green alike." These forces would soon be pressed into action in the first major engagement of the war, the Battle of Bull Run.

The First Battle of Bull Run
July 21, 1861

IN DEFENDING VIRGINIA, the Confederates took advantage of the lay of the land. Bounded to the east by the Potomac River and Chesapeake Bay, with riverways running east to west, the state offered ideal terrain to frustrate an overland advance southward from Washington. To the west the Blue Ridge Mountains and the Shenandoah Valley ran from southwest to northeast, meeting the Potomac at Harpers Ferry. Together the mountain range and the valley shielded troop movements that could easily threaten Washington and points north in Maryland and Pennsylvania, while the fertile valley could feed Virginia's defenders. For the moment, Confederate general Joseph E. Johnston with some 11,000 men checked one Union force just south of the Potomac, while to the east the hero of Fort Sumter, Pierre G. T. Beauregard, contested a potential Union advance by deploying his command, around 21,000 strong, along a small creek named Bull Run and a railroad junction at Manassas.

In mid-July McDowell decided to advance against Beauregard. The popular pressure was too much, and delay meant the loss of his initial influx of volunteer militia. Besides, with some 35,000 men under his command— the largest army ever directed by a United States general to date—he believed he would make short work of the Confederates defending Manassas. Word quickly leaked of the planned movement. Beauregard called for help: Johnston responded by entraining his men and headed toward Manassas.

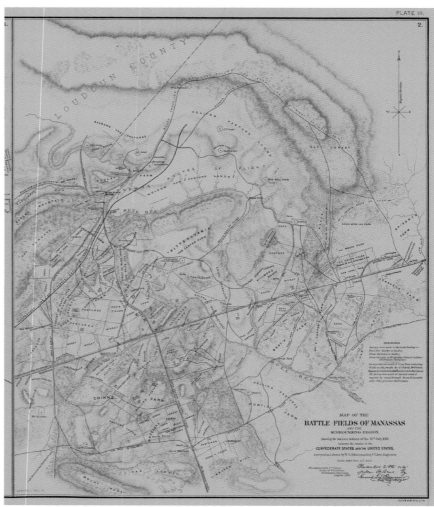

Union commander Robert Patterson was left with some 18,000 men in the dark. McDowell made contact with Beauregard on July 18 at Blackburn's Ford, and then sat back to plan his attack. He would march his men around the Confederate left flank, cross Bull Run, and descend upon

A map depicting the First Battle of Bull Run.

Union and Confederate forces clash at Manassas on July 21, 1861. It was the first major engagement of the war and exposed the weaknesses of the Union Army.

the enemy. Beauregard hatched a similar plan, targeting the Union left, but it was McDowell who struck first on the morning of July 21. A bevy of civilian onlookers had made their way down to Union lines from Washington, eager to witness what just might be the first—and last—major battle of the conflict.

McDowell's forces enjoyed early success, driving the Confederates southward toward a series of hills and ridges south of the Warrenton Turnpike. There rebel resistance stiffened. Johnston's men, having arrived at Manassas, hurried forward to stop the invading Yankees (as Northerners were dubbed), while a Virginia brigade under West Point graduate and Virginia Military Institute instructor Thomas J. Jackson

stood firm, inspiring another commander to cheer his men on: "There stands Jackson like a stone wall! Rally behind the Virginians!" The Union attack sputtered, and when the Confederates counterattacked that afternoon, the defenders dissolved and were routed from the battlefield. As the dispirited Yankees scrambled back to Washington, overwhelming the confused Washington civilians, Jefferson Davis arrived on the field and consulted with Beauregard and Johnston on the feasibility of pursuing the broken foe all the way to Washington. But the Confederates were as disorganized by their victory as the Union forces were by their defeat, and whatever opportunity there might have been quickly passed.

KEY FACTS: THE FIRST BATTLE OF BULL RUN, JULY 21, 1861 RESULT: CONFEDERATE VICTORY		
	Union	*Confederacy*
Units involved	Army of Northeastern Virginia	Army of the Potomac; Army of the Shenandoah
Commanders	Irvin McDowell	P. G. T. Beauregard
Total Forces	28,450	32,230
Casualties	2,896	1,982

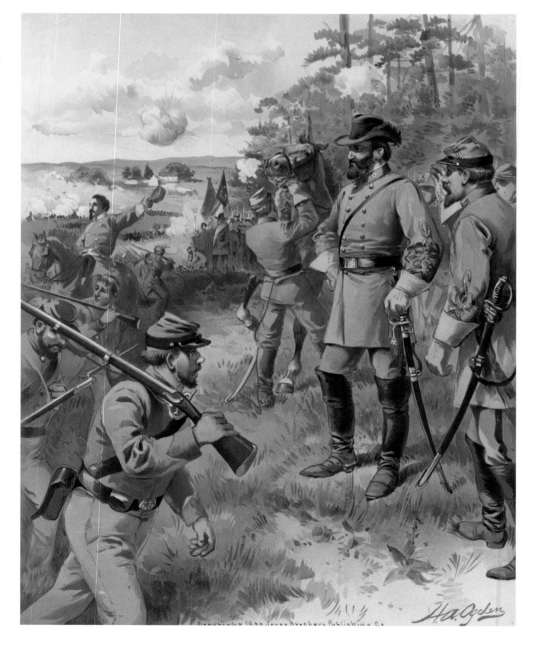

Thomas Jackson "stands like a stone wall" during a Union attack.

The confident Confederates claimed victory at what became known for a year as the battle of Manassas (for Southerners) or Bull Run (for Northerners). It had come at serious cost. More than 2,800 Union soldiers were killed, wounded, or missing, while the Confederates lost almost 2,000 men. The defeat and the ensuing disorganized retreat humiliated Union authorities and gave support to the theory that, man-for-man, the Confederates were superior fighters. But the psychological setback outweighed the military consequences. It did not take Union forces long to reorganize and refit under a new commander, George B. McClellan, who had made a name for himself in western Virginia by besting the Confederates in a series of small, sharp actions. McClellan looked the part of a general, so much so that his men and others compared him to Napoleon (both the famous former emperor and the current French leader). "I find myself in a new and strange position here," he wrote to his wife, with "Presdt, Cabinet, Genl Scott & all deferring to me—

Major General George McClellan distinguished himself by his conduct at the Battle of Bull Run. A few days later he was given command of the Army of the Potomac.

by some strange operation of magic I seem to have become the power of the land.... I almost think that were I to win some small success now I could become Dictator or anything else that might please me—but nothing of that kind would please me—therefore I won't be Dictator. Admirable self-denial!" Chastened by defeat, Lincoln and his supporters acceded to McClellan's demand that the general be given time to train his army, which soon bore the moniker the Army of the Potomac. Meanwhile, Confederate exuberance proved short-lived: before long strategic stalemate once more characterized operations in northern Virginia.

The Battle of Wilson's Creek on August 10, 1861 in Missouri proved an important Confederate victory.

Securing the Border States

The setback at Bull Run cast a long shadow over Union military operations. Weeks later, word came across the telegraph wire that on August 10 Nathaniel Lyon had been killed and his army defeated at Wilson's Creek in southwestern Missouri. Once more the Confederates were too disorganized by their triumph to take full advantage of the victory: while the battle inspired Missouri's Confederate supporters, it did little to shake Union control of the eastern part of the state.

If Lyon's haste had forced matters in Missouri, Union patience finally paid off in Kentucky. As September began, Confederate commander Leonidas Polk ordered the capture of Columbus, Kentucky, in order to block Union advances down the Mississippi River. Union brigadier general Ulysses S. Grant responded by seizing Paducah, thus securing control of the mouth of the Tennessee River, followed soon afterwards by taking the mouth of the Cumberland River as well. Polk's precipitous action tipped the balance in Kentucky against secession, capping weeks of building opposition to joining the Confederacy.

These movements revealed the importance of waterways in shaping military operations in the area west of the Appalachian Mountains westward across the Mississippi River Valley. It was easier for Union forces to move southward along the Mississippi, Tennessee, and Cumberland rivers than it was to attempt an overland campaign through Kentucky into Middle and East Tennessee, for the terrain to the east was more rugged and advancing forces would have to depend upon retaining control of roads and railroads to remain supplied. While a series of Confederate forts along the three western rivers sought to block Union advances, they proved vulnerable to capture from land, and Grant's aggressiveness meant that the Confederates would have to rely on a trio of Tennessee forts—Heiman, Henry, and Donelson—to block an advance along the Tennessee and Cumberland rivers.

Lincoln understood the importance of treating the issue of slavery cautiously while the fate of the

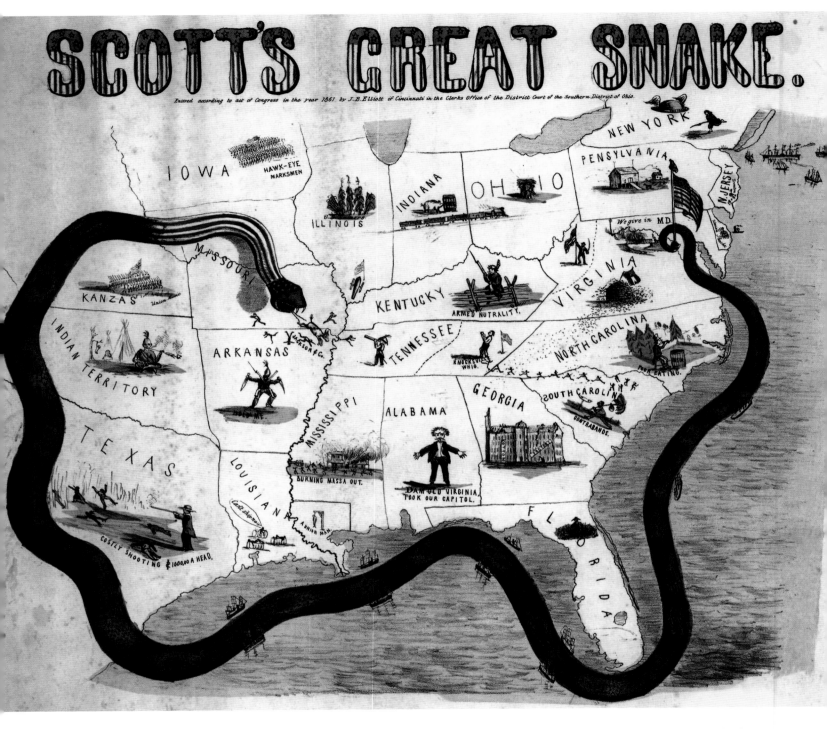

SCOTT'S GREAT SNAKE.

Entered according to act of Congress in the year 1861 by J.B. Elliott of Cincinnati in the Clerks Office of the District Court of the Southern District of Ohio.

border states was still up in the air. Responding to criticism of his decision to rescind Frémont's proclamation, he referred to the delicate balancing act that would determine Kentucky's allegiance. "I think to lose Kentucky is nearly the same as to lose the whole game," he remarked. "Kentucky gone, we can not hold Missouri, nor, as I think, Maryland. These all against us, and the job on our hands is too large for us." As he said, half in jest, "I hope to have God on my side, but I must have Kentucky."

Before long Lincoln also had Maryland, where a more aggressive approach carried the day.

General Winfield Scott's "Anaconda Plan" involved blockading the Southern ports while sending a force to secure the Mississippi River.

The Penn School, on St. Helena Island, South Carolina, was established by Laura Towne shortly after the Union Victory at Port Royal.

Although military force and martial law had secured communication and transportation links that ran through Baltimore to Washington, the allegiance of the rest of the state was still uncertain. Throughout most of the summer the Maryland legislature toyed with notions of neutrality but failed to take meaningful action; when the legislature convened in September, federal military authorities arrested pro-secessionist legislators, effectively ending any chance of the state joining the Confederacy.

Threatening the Confederate Perimeter

Securing control of essential areas of Missouri, Kentucky, and Maryland by the fall of 1861 proved far more important in the long run than did the Confederate victory at Manassas. Throughout the rest of the year minor Union offensives sought to uncover weak points in the Confederate defensive perimeter. The aging Union general-in-chief, Winfield Scott, outlined a potential plan for subduing the Confederacy. It featured an ever-tightening blockade of Confederate ports and a drive down the Mississippi to secure that critical waterway. Over time, Scott believed, the surrounded Confederates would feel economic pain and come to their senses without the war escalating to the point that it became destructive. Dubbed the "Anaconda Plan" because it looked as if snake-like Union forces were strangling the Confederacy, the plan proposed an obvious approach toward conquering the Confederacy but assumed that Southern whites' intransigence would be short-lived.

Scott never had a chance to implement his concept. For months George B. McClellan waged what might have been his most skillful campaign of the war to displace the Mexican–American War hero, whose age and obesity meant that he was confined to a desk in Washington. Eventually, McClellan carried the day and ascended to overall command of the armies of the United States on November 1, 1861. Yet the charismatic commander refused to launch an offensive southward. Believing that a single climactic large-scale battle would determine the war's outcome, McClellan wanted to train and reinforce his army so as to leave nothing to chance. Whether Lincoln, other members of the administration, congressional Republicans, or the public at large could wait so long was another matter entirely.

Only along the coasts did the Union make significant inroads during the remainder of the year. In November Union forces landed at Port Royal, South Carolina, located between Savannah, Georgia, and Charleston. Confederate resistance proved ineffective, although a series of fortified areas constructed under the supervision of Robert E. Lee blocked a Union advance inland. The victory provided the Union with a place to resupply vessels engaged in the blockade; it also presented Union military authorities with the challenge of addressing what to do with the sizable number of slaves abandoned by their masters in the area. Once more military operations had resulted in liberating slaves without regard for wider policy implications. For the moment the freed laborers would continue working the land, but now they earned wages, which eventually could fund land purchases. Teachers arrived to establish schools, and before long what became known as the Port Royal Experiment offered observers a glimpse into what black freedom might look like.

Union offensives also secured footholds along the North Carolina coast and captured Ship Island in the Gulf of Mexico, gaining yet another staging area for future military operations alongside Fort Pickens, near Pensacola, Florida, which remained in Union hands. These successes enhanced the prospects for a more effective blockade and offered places from which Union forces could launch offensives against targets along the Confederate coast, forcing the Confederates to use some of their precious manpower to protect their coastline.

This string of successes was threatened by a rash action undertaken by a Union naval officer. On November 7, Captain Charles Wilkes, commanding the USS *San Jacinto*, intercepted and boarded the RMS *Trent*, a British mail packet that happened to be carrying two Confederate diplomats headed to London and Paris. Wilkes took possession of the Confederates and let the *Trent* go on its way, but the damage had been done. Initial Northern jubilation over what appeared to be a signal success faded when news came that the British government viewed the boarding as a violation of Britain's status as neutral and a potential reason to go to war to uphold British rights and honor. The only way to avoid a confrontation would be if the United States released the diplomats. While Lincoln and his secretary of state, William Henry Seward, wanted to defend Wilkes's action, they admitted that the naval commander had acted on his own without orders, and should have seized the *Trent* and let a prize court determine the fate of the Confederate envoys. In the absence of such action, Lincoln and Seward agreed to release the prisoners, allowing them to continue to pursue their mission of securing European recognition and perhaps even intervention in or arbitration of the American conflict. Neither side wanted war, and both managed to work together to avoid it.

As 1861 came to a close, Union forces were poised to undertake offensive operations against the Confederacy. The disgrace and shame of the defeat at Bull Run had given way to a sense of optimism that victory might not be far off. For the Confederates, it was a period of watchful waiting and uncertainty about what would happen next. It would not be long until operations opened, although it came as a surprise as to who would strike the most telling blows.

The USS San Jacinto *and the RMS* Trent *face off, November 7, 1861. The confrontation worsened the relations between the Union and Great Britain and brought the two nations to the brink of war.*

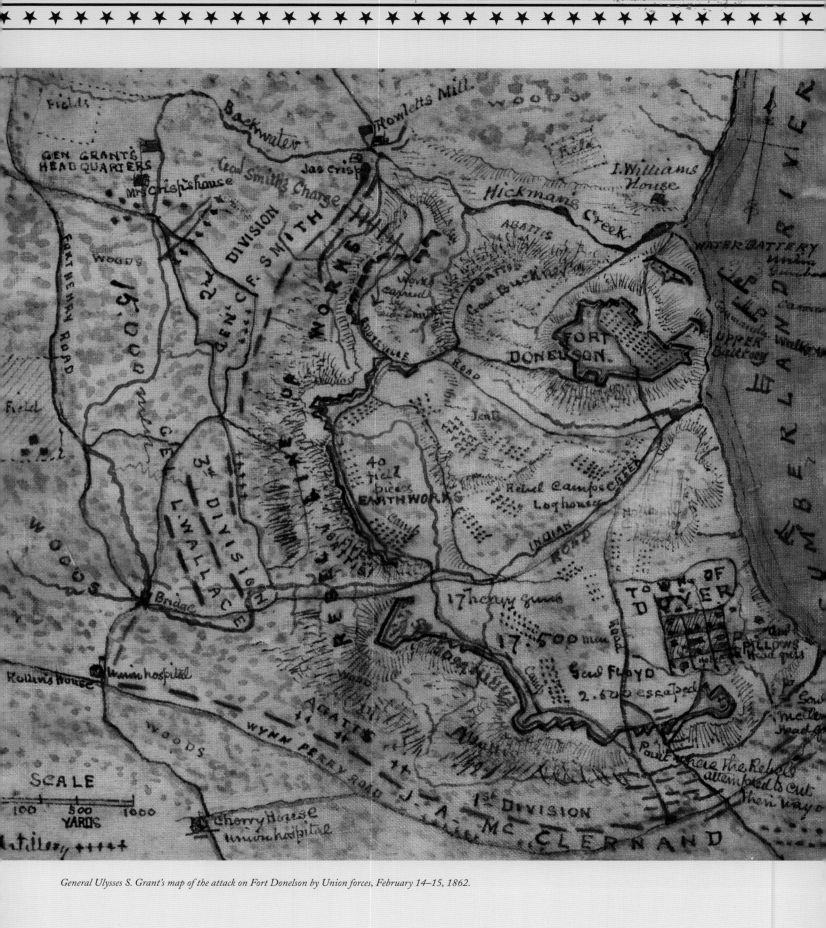

General Ulysses S. Grant's map of the attack on Fort Donelson by Union forces, February 14–15, 1862.

CHAPTER 3
THE LIMITS OF LIMITED WAR

As 1862 opened, Union forces stood poised to commence operations into the Confederate heartland. Most eyes focused on George B. McClellan's mighty army, ready to launch its long-awaited invasion of Virginia, with the Confederate capital at Richmond offering a tempting target. Yet it would not be McClellan's army that would capture attention. A sharp clash at Mill Springs, Kentucky, on January 19 suggested just how vulnerable the Confederate defensive perimeter in Kentucky and Tennessee might be. The next month Ulysses S. Grant confirmed that suspicion, and his advance opened the way for a series of Union successes along the Mississippi, Tennessee, and Cumberland rivers that threatened the Confederate territory.

The Emergence of Grant

Grant attracted little notice at the beginning of the war. Graduating in the middle of his class at West Point in 1843, he had served with distinction during the Mexican–American War of 1846–8. Peacetime military duty at a series of small posts had proved boring, however, and the young army officer, away from his family, began to drink … and could not hold his liquor. Resigning his captain's commission in 1854, he returned to his family, but struggled at several occupations as a civilian. At the outbreak of hostilities, he was working as a clerk in his father's general store in Galena, Illinois. It took him several months to

become a colonel of a volunteer regiment, and it was due to his congressman's influence that he won promotion to brigadier general. In November 1861 he tested Confederate defenses at Belmont, Missouri, just across the Mississippi River from the fortified Confederate position at Columbus, Kentucky. Initial success nearly turned into disaster when the Confederates counterattacked, but the engagement suggested to Grant that there must be some other way to break the Confederate line of defense. By early 1862 he had formulated a plan that featured advancing to capture Forts Heiman and Henry on the Tennessee River just south of Kentucky. A victory there would render Columbus vulnerable and force its evacuation while endangering Confederate possession of Nashville, the Tennessee state capital. At first Grant's superior, Henry Halleck, who had replaced Frémont in November 1861, demurred, but he relented when he heard rumors that the Confederates were shifting forces westward to reinforce their defenses.

In cooperation with a Union riverline flotilla of gunships and transports commanded by flag officer Andrew H. Foote, Grant advanced against Forts Henry and Heiman as February began. Heavy rains compromised the forts' integrity, and they fell without putting up much of a fight, as a Union gunship sailed inside Fort Henry. Grant then marched eastward to take Fort Donelson, located on the west bank of the Cumberland River.

It proved a tougher nut to crack; nevertheless, the commanders of the Confederate garrison decided to evacuate before Union reinforcements arrived. On February 15 they launched an attack on Grant's army designed to provide time and space for the garrison to make good its escape. Grant rallied his men, launched a counterattack, and benefited from the decision of the Confederate commanders to abandon their breakout attempt. That night Grant responded concisely to a request for surrender terms: "No terms except an unconditional and immediate surrender can be accepted. I propose to move immediately upon your works." The next day some 12,000 Confederates stacked arms and boarded transports that would take them north as prisoners of war.

The victories at Forts Henry, Heiman, and Donelson made Grant an instant national hero, hailed as "Unconditional Surrender Grant," a

Commodore Andrew Hull Foote led the Union flotilla against Forts Henry and Donelson.

Fort Henry was a critical strategic location on the Mississippi and Grant's successful attack on February 6, 1862, marked the first major victory for the Union in the Western Theater.

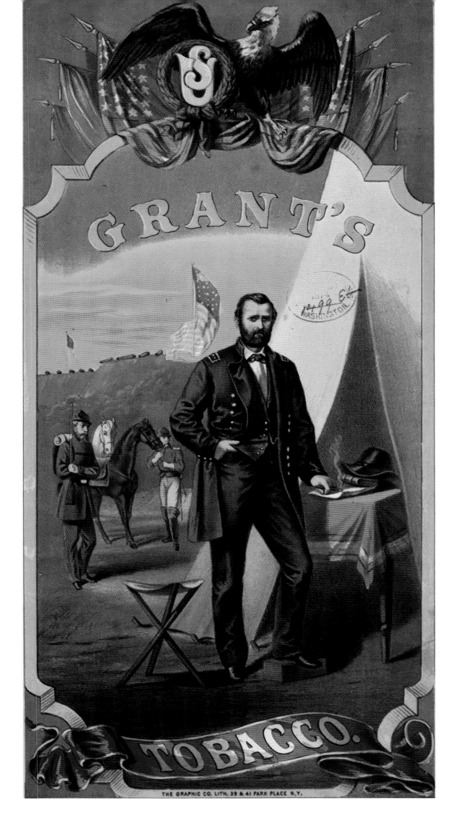

Grant's cigar-smoking habit became well known after his victories, and later his image was used as a promotional tool by various tobacco companies.

clever play on his initials. Hearing that the general had directed military operations with a cigar instead of a sword, a grateful public showered him with countless cigars, leaving the ever-pragmatic Grant to decide that the only way to dispose of the largesse was to commence puffing away (he would die some 23 years later of throat cancer). After nine days Union forces occupied Nashville; the Confederates abandoned Columbus, which some people had christened "the Gibraltar of the West," without a fight, opening a pathway for a Union advance southward along the Mississippi River. Before long Lincoln appointed Andrew Johnson military governor of the state. Chafing at his subordinate's success, Halleck took advantage of some administrative lapses to remove Grant from field command of his army and spread gossip that perhaps these shortcomings were due to Grant drinking again. However, he backed down when he came under pressure from the authorities in Washington to justify his action.

Grant rejoined his army at its encampment next to Pittsburgh Landing, a steamboat stage on the Tennessee River a short distance from the Mississippi state line. His force, known now as the Army of the Tennessee, had grown to over 40,000 men, including several divisions composed nearly entirely of raw recruits. Grant was under orders not to initiate further offensive operations but to await the arrival of fellow commander Don Carlos Buell, in charge of the Army of the Ohio; once the two armies joined forces, Halleck planned to take direct command in the field. Confederate commander Albert Sidney Johnston, still smarting from the series of setbacks suffered by his forces, planned to launch a surprise attack against Grant before Buell could arrive. Gathering an army nearly as strong as Grant's force, Johnston, with Pierre G. T. Beauregard serving as second-in-command, moved northward from Corinth, Mississippi, to deal Grant a devastating blow.

The Battle of Shiloh
April 6–7, 1862

S HILOH WAS THE bloodiest day of combat to date in United States history, with 13,000 Union and over 10,000 Confederate forces killed, wounded, or missing. Grant came under severe criticism for having failed to prepare for the possibility of a Confederate attack, and in months to come considered seeking a transfer or leaving the army altogether. As one Union officer put it, the army was not just surprised: "we were astonished."

Although the Confederate advance proved clumsy, the general in charge of reporting enemy activity, William T. Sherman, minimized signs of the rebel approach. After seeing combat as a brigade commander at Manassas, Sherman had been transferred to Kentucky, where he became so unnerved by what he believed to be the overwhelming task of subduing the Confederacy that he was replaced by Buell. Halleck had brought Sherman back as a division commander; his men were now encamped around Shiloh Church, southwest of the steamboat landing, although the area would prove anything but a place of peace. Afraid that any reports of enemy activity would give rise to rumors that his wild imagination was a sign of mental instability, Sherman discounted them, and Grant accepted his reports at face value. Thus it was something of a surprise, to say the least, when on April 6, Palm Sunday, the Confederates commenced their attack just as most of the Yankees were preparing breakfast.

Although Union forces along the encampment's perimeter quickly engaged the advancing Confederates, before long the Yankees found themselves retreating, with some soldiers running away to seek safety by the bluffs near the steamship landing. Once Grant arrived on the field, be began to coordinate defensive operations. He was confident that he would soon receive reinforcements, for the lead elements of Buell's command, some 18,000 strong, were within earshot. Through the day, however, the Confederates continued to advance, at one point compelling Union general Benjamin Prentiss to surrender what remained of his division when it was virtually surrounded. But the exhausted Confederates suffered serious losses themselves, including Johnston, who bled to death from a

Despite his military successes in Virginia, P. G. T. Beauregard found himself second-in-command at Shiloh to Albert Sidney Johnston.

The Battle of Shiloh was a brutal affair that brought to light the human cost of the Civil War.

bullet wound in his leg. As Beauregard ascended to command, he decided that he would renew the battle in the morning, confident that he could deliver a final blow. He did not count on Grant being reinforced, nor did he anticipate that it would be Grant who would attack first on the morning of April 7. By the end of the day it would be the Confederates who were in full retreat while the Yankees found themselves too bloodied and exhausted to mount a forceful pursuit.

Nevertheless the Union prevailed at Shiloh; days later it triumphed once more with the capture of Island No. 10 along the Mississippi River. As planned, Halleck consolidated his armies, advanced methodically upon Corinth, and entered the city on the heels of a Confederate evacuation on May 30, 1862. A week later Memphis also fell to Union forces, and West Tennessee was in Union hands, and soon after New Orleans had fallen, too.

KEY FACTS:
THE BATTLE OF SHILOH, APRIL 6–7, 1862
RESULT: UNION VICTORY

	Union	Confederacy
Units involved	Army of the Tennessee; Army of the Ohio	Army of Mississippi
Commanders	Ulysses S. Grant and Don Carlos Buell	Albert Sidney Johnson
Total Forces	65,085	44,968
Casualties	13,047	10,669

McClellan on the Move

The success of Union arms in the west in the winter of 1862 stood in stark contrast to the continuing stalemate in the east. "All quiet along the Potomac," a saying which once recognized McClellan's achievement of restoring order in the wake of defeat, now took on a more derisive tone. As the new year began, Lincoln began to lose patience with his general, who initially refused to share his plans with his superiors. Faced with a minimum of activity across all fronts, the president on January 27 issued an order directing Union armies to advance by Washington's birthday, which would also be the day Jefferson Davis took office as the first elected president of the Confederacy. The victories at Mill Springs and Forts Henry and Donelson, as well as Ambrose Burnside's efforts along the North Carolina seacoast, brought into sharper relief McClellan's inactivity.

Part of the problem was due to the fact that McClellan favored taking advantage of the Potomac River and Chesapeake Bay to transport his men south over water to threaten Richmond from one of the many rivers that flowed westward through tidewater Virginia. Lincoln noted that such an approach might render Washington vulnerable to attack, especially from Confederate forces lurking in the Shenandoah Valley or northern Virginia. The president preferred an overland approach that would shield Washington as much as it threatened Richmond; moreover, he believed that it was of the utmost importance to engage the enemy's armies to achieve victory. Although McClellan complied with Lincoln's wishes and advanced against the fortified Confederate position at Manassas, he found it abandoned and returned to Washington. He then pressed for the adoption of his plan. Lincoln finally acceded, but required McClellan to leave behind a force sufficient to defend Washington. He also stripped the responsibilities of general-in-chief from McClellan, feeling that perhaps the general's attention had been divided without much result.

As McClellan advocated for his plan, panic seized Washington when news came that the Confederates

had launched a new fighting vessel, clad in iron, that could take punishment while reducing wooden frigates to splinters. For months Confederate shipbuilders in Norfolk (in Portsmouth, Virginia) had labored to construct such a vessel over what

The USS Monitor *and the* CSS Virginia *square off in the Battle of Hampton Roads, the first engagement between two ironclads.*

remained of the hull of a steam-powered wooden frigate, the USS *Merrimack*. Christened the CSS *Virginia*, it carried 12 guns and brandished a ram. Sailing out into Hampton Roads on March 8, it made short work of two Union vessels and prepared to return the next day to finish off a third. Rumors circulated that once the *Virginia* finished its work, it would steam northward and head for Washington, although in truth it was not seaworthy enough for such an operation.

When the *Virginia* reappeared the next day, a strange-looking vessel, likened to a "cheesebox on a raft," awaited its arrival. This was the USS *Monitor*, an ironclad ship built in the Brooklyn Navy Yard, which featured two guns mounted inside a rotating turret. After some two hours of inconclusive combat the vessels broke off, with the *Virginia* returning to the Norfolk Navy Yard. Although it would sally forth again in limited fashion, it never again engaged the Union fleet, including the *Monitor*. But naval warfare was forever transformed, although the careful student will note that the British and French governments had also invested in the development of ironclad ships prior to the Civil War.

While Washington was now secure against attack from the sea, Lincoln still feared that the capital was vulnerable from land. As McClellan embarked his men aboard transports headed toward the York and James rivers, news arrived that a small Confederate force under the general now known as Stonewall Jackson had struck at Union forces in the Shenandoah Valley at Kernstown near Winchester, Virginia. Concerned that Harpers Ferry and Washington might be vulnerable to a Confederate attack, Lincoln directed McClellan to leave behind a significant number of infantry units; he then learned that McClellan did not plan to leave behind as many men as Lincoln deemed sufficient to protect Washington. McClellan protested in vain: so long as Jackson remained as a distraction in the Shenandoah, he would continue to attract Lincoln's attention and detract from McClellan's anticipated strength.

At the end of March, McClellan began moving the Army of the Potomac by sea to Fort Monroe, Virginia, where the James and York rivers emptied into Chesapeake Bay. Advancing toward Yorktown, he halted before the Confederate fortifications defending the city. Although he outnumbered the

defenders, he chose to wait until he could bring overwhelming numbers to bear in an assault. Before he could attack in early May, however, the Confederate commander, Joseph E. Johnston, ordered a withdrawal, abandoning Yorktown and temporarily checking a Yankee pursuit at Williamsburg. Days later Union forces secured the mouth of the James River by taking Norfolk, causing the Confederates to blow up the CSS *Virginia*. McClellan could thus proceed westward toward Richmond with his flanks secured.

McClellan's optimism was tempered by his failure to secure reinforcements from the forces defending Washington. This was largely due to Stonewall Jackson's continued presence in the Shenandoah Valley. Jackson used the terrain to his advantage, blocking access to the valley through its

OPPOSITE: A map showing the arrangement of Union and Confederate fortifications around Yorktown in April 1862. Yorktown was an important point en route to the Confederate capital of Richmond, but McClellan's hesitation gave the Southerners time to regroup.

BELOW: A map of the Battle of Kernstown. The battle was the first of Stonewall Jackson's Shenandoah campaign.

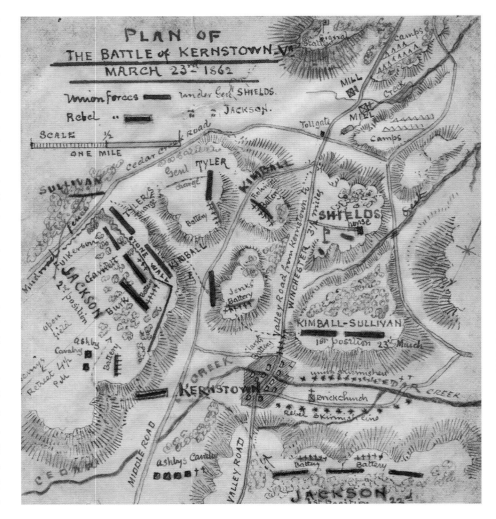

MAP OF THE LINES AT YORKTOWN VIRGINIA. April. 1862.

FROM OFFICIAL MAPS and Reconnoisances and Surveys made between 3rd and 30th April 1862. by U.S. Engineers under Col Alexander M⁰
Maj Humphreys Capt W⁰ Keine. R K Sneden and others   Copy from Map made for Maj Gen¹ Sam¹ P. Heintzelman U.S.A. Comand⁹ 3ʳᵈ Corps A. P.
Drawn at Head qrs at the "Sawmill"
by R K Sneden
Top. Eng.

Note.
YORKTOWN was evacuated
on night of 3ʳᵈ May 1862. rear
guard left at daylight of 4ᵗʰ
when the whole Rebel
army fell back to the
Entrenched position at
WILLIAMSBURG

Road to Williamsburg   12 miles

WINDMILL CREEK

GLOUCESTER POINT BATTERIES

YORKTOWN and 125 Guns

GLOCESTER POINT

U.S. Gunboats Shelling

Galena   Port Royal
Aroostook

Bordan's Sharpshooters

Peach Orchard

McCall No 10

WORMSLEY CREEK

Mouth of Wormsley Creek

Fitz John Porter
5ᵗʰ Reg Cavalry

Head Qurt Gen¹ McClellan

Reserve Artillery Park

U.S. Signal Corps

3ʳᵈ CORPS HEINTZELMAN

HOWES SAWMILL in operation

CLARKES House
Union Hospitals

Gen¹ HOOKER Corps

6ᵗʰ CORPS SEDGWICK

WARWICK Court House

Birney
Kearny

Reference.

Union Forces and Works
Confederate Forces and Works

Pickets   artillery   Cavalry
Union Army 85,000 men
Cavalry. 11,200 men in all of Magruder's
Command

Union Works

Total Armament of Batteries
62 guns. 39 mortars.
Field Batteries. A. B. C and D
Length of front of Union Defenses 7 miles
Length of Confederate Defense 13 miles
Glocester to James River.
Union Army now
was 140,000 of all arms
Of whom 28,000 died in C

passes while he struck at one Federal column, then another, all the while continuing to pose a threat to Washington. Hoping to track Jackson down and destroy him altogether, Lincoln redirected reinforcements earmarked for McClellan to join in the campaign against the wily rebel, meaning that Jackson was able to distract an enemy force much larger than his own. McClellan fumed and complained. Failing to augment his force to what he believed was its necessary strength, he advanced deliberately up the peninsula between the York and James rivers; Johnston continued to withdraw in the face of superior numbers, until he was but a handful of miles outside Richmond. Just as McClellan was aware of Lincoln's impatience with the slow pace of operations, Johnston grew increasingly cognizant of Jefferson Davis's desire to strike a blow to defend the Confederate capital.

At the end of May, Johnston finally launched an attack against McClellan at Fair Oaks (also known as Seven Pines). It seemed an ideal opportunity to damage McClellan, because his army was divided, with the Chickahominy River separating the two wings. But Johnston failed to dislodge the Federals; moreover, he was severely wounded. To replace him Davis decided upon his military adviser, Robert E. Lee.

Lee Takes Command

Robert E. Lee's record of achievement during the first year of the war was mixed at best. His first experience in the field in western Virginia proved a failure, and he was unable to reverse Union successes. Transferred to the South Atlantic coast, he helped to stem Union advances inland from their coastal strongholds; he then became Jefferson Davis's adviser in Richmond, where his most significant contribution was to support Jackson's operations. This was not a bright beginning for an officer many believed showed great promise. Nor were observers encouraged when Lee's first decision upon taking command of what was already known as the Army of Northern Virginia was to prepare fortified positions to resist McClellan's advance while reinforcements were still being withheld from McClellan due to the continued active presence of Jackson in the valley.

Lee was not content to await McClellan's next move. He ordered the construction of fortifications so that he could hold his lines with fewer men, thus allowing him to concentrate a force strong enough to strike a blow at McClellan. He then authorized cavalry commander James

J. E. B. Stuart was an effective cavalry commander and he had fought in the frontier conflicts of Bleeding Kansas in the 1850s.

OPPOSITE: A map showing the troop movements during the Seven Days' Battles.

BELOW LEFT: Captain John Tidball with his artillery at the Battle of Fair Oaks.

BELOW: General Robert E. Lee, the Confederacy's most celebrated commander.

Ewell Brown "Jeb" Stuart to take his horsemen on a ride around McClellan's army in order to gather information, interrupt communications and supplies, and keep McClellan off-balance. This done, Lee, after first pretending to reinforce Jackson, ordered Jackson to join Lee's army outside Richmond, where it would attack what remained of McClellan's right flank north of the Chickahominy River. If Lee could bring the Federals to battle piece by piece, he might prevail through superior numbers at the point of attack.

Stuart's ride around the Union army alerted McClellan to the vulnerability of his supply line via the York River, and so he made plans to shift his base of operations southward to the James, which was far more secure. However, he still kept part of his army north of the Chickahominy, in part to protect his shift of base and to link up with any reinforcements that might march southward from Fredericksburg, less than 50 miles away. Those long-awaited reinforcements, which McClellan deemed essential to ensure the success of his operations, never arrived. Instead, Lee moved forward on June 25, striking McClellan's exposed right flank, and commenced a series of battles designed to drive the Army of the Potomac away from Richmond as well as to damage if not decisively defeat it. In a series of clashes collectively known as the Seven Days' Battles, Lee achieved the former

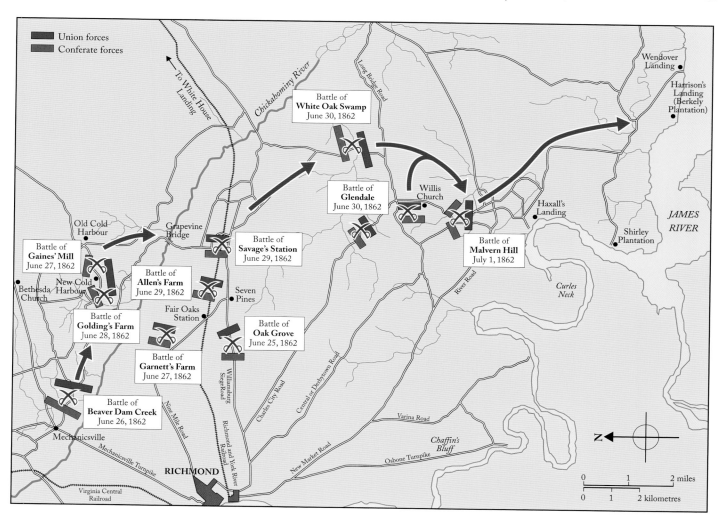

but fell short of the latter, as McClellan's commanders waged a fighting withdrawal that ended on July 1 when Lee launched a series of futile assaults upon a well-prepared defender at Malvern Hill, just north of the James. Both sides suffered sizable losses, but Richmond was no longer under immediate threat.

Although Lee had managed to drive McClellan away from the immediate proximity of Richmond, the Army of the Potomac, should it take the offensive, was still perfectly capable of threatening the Confederate capital. However, the Southern triumph put an end to dreams of a quick end to the war and ensured that if it continued, its scope would broaden as it escalated. The Northern public had placed a great deal of confidence in George B. McClellan's ability to prevail, but it was disappointed. As Lincoln pointed out a few weeks later, "The moral effect was the worst of the affair before Richmond; and that has run its course downward; we are now at a stand, and shall soon be rising again, as we hope. I believe it is true that in men and material, the enemy suffered more than we, in that series of conflicts; while it is certain he is less able to bear it."

The Trans-Mississippi

Most Americans and Europeans tended to focus their attention on the progress of the war in the eastern theater, especially Virginia followed by Maryland and Pennsylvania. The proximity of Richmond and Washington added to the theater's allure. They tended to glance more briefly at events between the Appalachians and the Mississippi, although newspapers in Cincinnati and Chicago made sure that the region was not neglected.

The Battle of Malvern Hill on July 1, 1862, was the last of the Seven Days Battles and saw more than 100,000 men in action.

An M1840 sword used in the Civil War. These weapons were carried by non-commissioned officers throughout the course of the war.

West of the Mississippi, however, far fewer people followed the movements of much smaller armies seeking to gain control of the American southwest. Yet from the beginning of the conflict some Confederates saw the opportunity to extend their new nation westward, perhaps all the way to California. One did not know what natural resources might be discovered, much as the discovery of gold in California in 1848 had come as something of a surprise. Should the Confederacy reach all the way to the Pacific coast, it could take advantage of new trading opportunities. Many white Americans, claiming that the government in Washington had neglected their interests, thought that Richmond might treat them better; others took a renewed look at Mexico as either an opportunity for expansion or a possible threat, depending on the outcome of a French-directed military intervention there. Union forces sought to protect their links eastward toward the rest of the United States.

A cannonball from the Battle of Glorieta Pass.

Confederate sympathizers in the southwestern portion of the New Mexico Territory, commonly known as Arizona, attempted to establish their own government in 1861. By February 1862 Confederate forces were marching westward to try to secure the southern portion of the New Mexico Territory, including Arizona, for the Confederacy. Union forces checked this effort at Glorieta Pass in March; the following month Confederates failed to stop the advancing Yankees at Picacho Pass, north of the Confederate territorial capital at Tucson, and they abandoned their efforts to secure the region.

Union forces also scored successes in Missouri, Arkansas, and Louisiana. Recovering from defeats at Wilson's Creek and the ensuing siege of Lexington, both in western Missouri, Union forces under General Samuel R. Curtis advanced southward across the state in the late winter of 1862, crossing into Arkansas. At Pea Ridge, the Confederates launched a counteroffensive, initially forcing back the Union defenders, but ultimately they failed to drive Curtis away. Although guerrilla operations in Missouri proved vicious, Confederates never again seriously contested Union control of the state. The Union occupation of New Orleans the following month shut off the Mississippi to the Confederates, who saw their control of the river dwindle to the western border of Mississippi and northern Louisiana, preserved largely by their continued occupation of Vicksburg, which repelled a naval attack in July 1862.

Once more, however, Union triumphs in the west were overshadowed by setbacks in Virginia. A decisive victory remained elusive, largely because people looked for it in the area where the two national capitals stood. As Lincoln put it in August, "it seems unreasonable that a series of successes, extending through half-a-year and clearing more

than a hundred thousand square miles of country, should help us so little, while a single half-defeat should hurt us so much. But let us be patient." The patience the president sought might be in short supply, however: Lincoln needed some way to rally support for the war effort.

Escalation

When the American Civil War broke out in 1861, the vast majority of Union military commanders embraced the notion of limiting the conflict to a war between armies. Civilians should not be the targets of military operations, and private property should be respected as much as possible. To broaden the scope of the war would spark intensified resistance among Confederate civilians, rendering reconciliation problematic.

These principles eroded as armies marched down dusty dirt roads and through small towns. Soldiers ripped apart fences for firewood, looked to local farms to augment their food rations, and did not always respect civilians' desire to be left alone, especially when those same civilians seemed hostile to the soldiers' presence. Enslaved blacks took the opportunity offered by the proximity of Union soldiers and the disorder that accompanied their advance to escape their bondage, infuriating white Southerners still more. Through early 1862, however, most Union commanders looked to limit the impact of military operations upon surrounding civilians, except when their farms and fields turned into bloody battlefields or were refashioned into forts, camps, and entrenchments.

Hopes that the war would be short and reconciliation easily accomplished faded in 1862. Confederate military setbacks did not diminish the determination of most Confederate civilians to persist in their support for a war for Southern independence, even if they were not always willing to make the material and human sacrifices that accompanied such resistance. Some Union soldiers, encountering the reality of slavery for the first time, became convinced of its inhumanity; others despised the efforts of white Southerners to employ enslaved blacks in direct support of the Confederate war effort. Union commanders such as Grant and Sherman witnessed the persistence of Confederate civilian resistance as they embarked on occupation duty in West Tennessee in the wake of Yankee triumphs at Shiloh and Corinth; so did John Pope, who brought his attitudes east with him in June 1862 when Lincoln appointed him to take charge of the various Union commands in northern Virginia and form them into the Army of Virginia just as Lee opened his offensive against McClellan. In a series of orders, Pope directed his men to live off the land, taking food and horses from local civilians,

Brigadier General John Pope was infamous for his harsh treatment of the civilian population in the occupied territories in the Western Theater, and he brought his controversial approach with him when ordered to Virginia.

Order No. 11 in 1863 forced inhabitants in Missouri to prove their loyalty or face deportation. Similar measures were taken throughout the West to discourage civilian resistance by Confederate sympathizers.

and outlined harsh measures to counter guerrilla activity, including holding civilians responsible for such actions. Civilians would have to take loyalty oaths to the United States or face arrest; violations of said oaths constituted grounds for individuals' removal or execution and confiscation of property. Such orders echoed similar directives issues by commanders elsewhere, but Pope's proximity to Washington gave his measures wide publicity. They also infuriated Confederate leaders and civilians.

Back at Harrison's Landing, George B. McClellan took advantage of a visit by Abraham Lincoln to voice his objection to escalation. The military conflict "should not be a War looking to the subjugation of the people of any state, in any event. It should not be, at all, a War upon population; but

against armed forces and political organizations. Neither confiscation of property, political executions of persons, territorial organization of states or forcible abolition of slavery should be contemplated for a moment." Otherwise, reconciliation would be difficult, perhaps impossible; moreover, McClellan observed, "A declaration of radical views, especially upon slavery, will rapidly disintegrate our present Armies."

Lincoln thanked McClellan for his missive, and quietly pocketed the letter. Perhaps he had tired of taking advice from a general whose inability to secure a decisive victory meant that the war would drag on, thus raising the issue of whether the Union should escalate the conflict in order to prevail. Pope's orders pointed in that direction; so did the increasing debate over what to do about slavery.

Abraham Lincoln, General John McClernand and E. J. Allen, Chief of the Secret Service, meet at the headquarters of the Army of the Potomac near Antietam, October 4, 1862.

CHAPTER 4
ESCALATION AND EMANCIPATION

VISIONS OF A QUICK and easy conflict faded rapidly in the aftermath of Lee's triumph over McClellan east of Richmond, as the complexities of the war became more obvious and more intense. That the same United States Congress which in July 1861 passed the Johnson-Crittenden Resolution to exclude the destruction of slavery from United States war aims would only weeks later approve legislation that rendered slaves used by the Confederacy for military purposes vulnerable to being seized as contraband of war by Union military authorities highlighted the tension between the goals of the war, its conduct, and the consequences of how both sides conducted military operations.

Among those observers who reluctantly saw how the conflict was transforming the republic that both sides sought to protect was Abraham Lincoln. Although he had denounced slavery as both immoral and a violation of the vision of the republic's founding fathers, he wrestled with how best to address the situation and set the "peculiar institution" on the road to ultimate extinction. One approach that found favor

A group of "contrabands" at Cumberland Landing, Virginia, May 14, 1862.

with him, propounded by his political hero, Henry Clay, called for the gradual elimination of slavery, provided for the compensation of masters who surrendered title to their slaves, and sought the voluntary relocation of both free and freed blacks outside the United States. Such an approach would address the issues of lost property and capital that concerned slaveholders; it would also mollify those whites whose racial prejudices prevented them from accepting a post-emancipation multiracial society, which inspired so much fear and anger among so many American whites. A gradual emancipation would cushion white Americans from the impact of sudden and immediate change. In short, although such a plan would free slaves and end slavery, it was primarily framed with the interests of white Americans in mind. It became a particular passion with the president, who was well aware of the ways in which white prejudice would compromise the prospects for black freedom even as he dealt with his own complicated feelings on the matter. A free republic would be largely a white republic: slavery would disappear without forcing white Americans to contemplate the prospect of a multiracial United States.

In December 1861, Lincoln set forth his case for gradual and compensated emancipation followed by colonization in his first annual message to Congress. He asked whether the adoption of his approach amounted to an "absolute necessity … without which the government itself cannot be perpetuated?" Such strong language suggested the depth of his commitment to the plan and how central it was to his vision of eventual victory. "In considering the policy to be adopted for suppressing the insurrection," he remarked, "I have been anxious and careful that the inevitable conflict for this purpose shall not degenerate into a violent and remorseless revolutionary struggle." Thus the president presented his proposed policy as a conservative measure to forestall far more chaotic and far-reaching alternatives. He pledged "to keep the integrity of the Union prominent as the primary object of the contest on our part, leaving all questions which are not of vital

Abraham Lincoln argued for gradual emancipation, but insisted that the war was not about slavery but about preserving the integrity of the Union.

military importance to the more deliberate action of the legislature." Thus emancipation, however achieved, was a means to an end, never quite an end in itself.

Military affairs and congressional legislation soon outpaced the president's preference for a more deliberate approach. As Union forces advanced southward, they encountered a growing number of escaping slaves seeking sanctuary within Yankee lines. The numbers promised to prove overwhelming for a military not prepared to care for refugees and uncertain as to how to handle them. Congress simplified such matters when in March 1862 it directed military commanders not to return slaves to their masters, regardless of the situation or the political sentiments of the owner. Four months later, in the wake of McClellan's defeat before Richmond, Congress passed a second confiscation act, this time declaring free all slaves held by secessionist masters. This measure went far beyond the First Confiscation Act: it no longer mattered whether the enslaved people were being used explicitly in support of the Confederate war effort, and it liberated those people rather than holding that the federal government had assumed title to them. The momentum and friction of conflict led to its escalation: the war to save the Union was transforming it, while the

Fugitive slaves cross the Rappahanock river in 1862. Many slaves sought out the protection of the Union Army, but their position was ambiguous and many were returned to their former masters.

Confederacy's war to protect slavery rendered the "peculiar institution" vulnerable to the vicissitudes of military conflict.

In such matters Lincoln followed rather than led, although he made sure that no one moved too far ahead of him. He reminded military commanders that they were not to make policy but to implement it. John C. Frémont had learned that lesson the hard way in 1861 when Lincoln rescinded Frémont's orders freeing slaves of pro-secessionist Missouri slaveholders. In April 1862 it was Major General David Hunter's turn. He issued orders that provided for the emancipation of slaves in his department, which included South Carolina, Georgia, and Florida, although Union forces had not advanced far beyond their coastal footholds. In May Lincoln revoked Hunter's proclamation,

reminding everyone that such decisions rested in his hands—which conceded that he now believed he had the power to strike at slavery, but awaited events to see whether it would be wise to do so.

What had changed in Lincoln's thinking was his acceptance that he might find constitutional justification for striking against slavery, based upon his assessment of military necessity, which drew upon a very expansive interpretation of the implications inherent in the president's so-called war powers. That the Constitution never used those words but simply provided for presidential control of military personnel and operations as commander-in-chief was something for others to argue. Once Lincoln decided that in order to subdue the Confederacy he needed to strike at slavery, he believed he had the constitutional justification to act. What restrained him for the moment was his persisting belief that white Southern Unionists might take the lead in paving a path toward reunion, while Confederate resistance would subside in the face of military setbacks coupled with a realization that Lincoln did not seek to destroy slavery as a matter of policy.

These hopeful assumptions perished in the face of reality. Union military advances secured territory where support for secession remained strong, especially in areas where slaveholding was widespread. The areas where Unionism was strongest—along the Appalachian Mountain chain that brought together western Virginia, western North Carolina, East Tennessee, and slices of northern Alabama—remained elusive and distant. Southern Unionists dared not expose themselves to potential retaliation without the promise of secure Union occupation that would withstand Confederate attempts to regain control. Moreover, the territorial scope of Union occupation in states such as North Carolina and Louisiana was limited, frustrating efforts to project civil authority beyond boundaries established by bayonets.

McClellan's failure to take Richmond signaled to Lincoln that escalation through emancipation had become a matter of military necessity. He had lost faith in the willingness of Southern white Unionists to act. He had tired of their fearfulness, complaining that "this class of men will do nothing for the government, nothing for themselves, except demanding that the government shall not strike its open enemies, lest they be struck by accident!" As he told Reverdy Johnson, a Maryland Unionist, he well understood white Southern Unionists' fears of abolition and its ensuing chaos. "They very well know the way to avert all this is simply to take their place in the Union upon the old terms," Lincoln observed. "If they will not do this, should they not receive harder blows rather than lighter ones?" Inaction was inadvisable. The president's patience was running out. "What would you do in my position?" he asked one Southern Unionist. "Would you drop the war where it is? Or, would you prosecute it in future, with elder-stalk squirts, charged with rose water? Would you deal lighter

blows rather than heavier ones? Would you give up the contest, leaving any available means unapplied[?]" The answer was obvious. "I must save this government if possible," he told Johnson. "What I cannot do, of course I will not do; but it may as well be understood, once for all, that I shall not surrender this game leaving any available card unplayed."

Still, the president remained wedded to his preference for gradual emancipation, compensation for masters, and the voluntary relocation of the freed outside the United States. Weeks after discussing the possibility of emancipation with his cabinet, he invited a delegation of black ministers to the White House to make his case once more. Lincoln

Major General David Hunter issued an emancipation order in South Carolina, Georgia, and Florida in April 1862 which was soon revoked.

The first page of Lincoln's letter revoking Hunter's emancipation proclamation.

went so far as to suggest that the presence of black slaves (as opposed to the actions of whites in deciding to enslave fellow human beings in the first place) was at the root of the conflict, adding that whites' prejudice against blacks was so strong and enduring that it might be best if blacks emigrated elsewhere for their own good. However, few blacks responded to Lincoln's logic: after all, they pointed out, those whites who wanted blacks to return whence they came overlooked the fact that the vast majority of American slaves had been born in the United States. Without slaveholders willing to sell their slaves and with few blacks willing to emigrate, Lincoln's vision of colonization was doomed.

To *New York Tribune* newspaper editor Horace Greeley, who pressed Lincoln to strike at slavery, the president made clear his policy:

I would save the Union. I would save it the shortest way under the Constitution. The sooner the national authority can be restored; the nearer the Union will be "the Union as it was." If there be those who would not save the Union, unless they could at the same time save slavery, I do not agree with them. If there be those who would not save the Union unless they could at the same time destroy slavery, I do not agree with them. My paramount object in this struggle is to save the Union, and is not either to save or to destroy slavery. If I could save the Union without freeing any slave I would do it, and if I could save it by freeing all the slaves I would do it; and if I could save it by freeing some and leaving others alone I would also do that. What I do about slavery, and the colored race, I do because I believe it helps to save the Union; and what I forbear, I forbear because I do not believe it would help to save the Union. I shall do less whenever I shall believe what I am doing hurts the cause, and I shall do more whenever I shall believe doing more will help the cause. I shall try to correct errors when shown to be errors; and I shall adopt new views so fast as they shall appear to be true views.

Lest Greeley or anyone else labor under any confusion about the president's attitude toward slavery, Lincoln added: "I have here stated my purpose according to my view of official duty; and I intend no modification of my oft-expressed personal wish that all men every where could be free."

The summer of 1862 proved to be a time of reckoning for Lincoln. His hopes that resurgent white Unionism in the South would counter commitment to the Confederacy proved illusory, a wild underestimation of just how determined most Confederates were to establish an independent republic that would safeguard slavery forever. The promise of a quick victory presaged by Union victories in Kentucky and Tennessee and along the Mississippi River faded in the wake of McClellan's failure to take Richmond. The president found himself virtually alone on his preferred path to emancipation and colonization, a cherished notion that found few takers. Things were not going well for the embattled chief executive, and there seemed to be no end in sight.

Confederate Counteroffensives

As Lincoln mulled what to do about colonization, Confederate armies moved northward through Virginia, Tennessee, and Mississippi in a massive if uncoordinated counteroffensive to take back Union gains. Once reassured that McClellan's Army of the Potomac was departing from its James River defenses, thus no longer posing an immediate threat to Richmond, Robert E. Lee hurried north to strike hard at John Pope's Army of Virginia before McClellan could reinforce it. Lee and his lieutenants Jackson, Longstreet, and Stuart drove Pope back from central Virginia, devastated the Union supply depot at Manassas Junction, and then took position north and west of the old Bull Run battlefield in order to lure Pope into combat. For days Pope, reinforced by advance elements of McClellan's army, attempted to drive the Confederates away, eventually focusing upon Jackson's position along an unfinished railroad cut, before Longstreet's divisions smashed into the virtually undefended Union left flank and came close to sweeping the Yankees from

the battlefield altogether. That Pope escaped with most of his force intact may have seemed to be something of a miracle, but it bore testimony to the virtual indestructibility of Civil War armies on the battlefield proper.

Lee decided to take the war north of the Potomac River. Perhaps Marylanders sympathetic to the Confederacy might finally be sufficiently inspired to secede; Confederate military success might tip the balance in favor of European intervention; and the Northern electorate might decide it was time to abandon the Lincoln administration and the Republican Party. The way seemed clear to deliver a devastating blow, for McClellan confronted forming a field army out of the disparate elements of Pope's army, his own army now arrived from the James River, and various other scattered forces. Lee believed that McClellan's deliberate and cautious nature would allow the Confederates ample time to carry out their assignments, including the capture of the sizable Union garrison at Harpers Ferry.

That Lincoln entrusted McClellan to bring order out of chaos in the wake of Pope's defeat

Horace Greeley, editor of the New York Tribune, was a fierce advocate for abolition.

A map showing the arrangement of forces in the Second Battle of Bull Run.

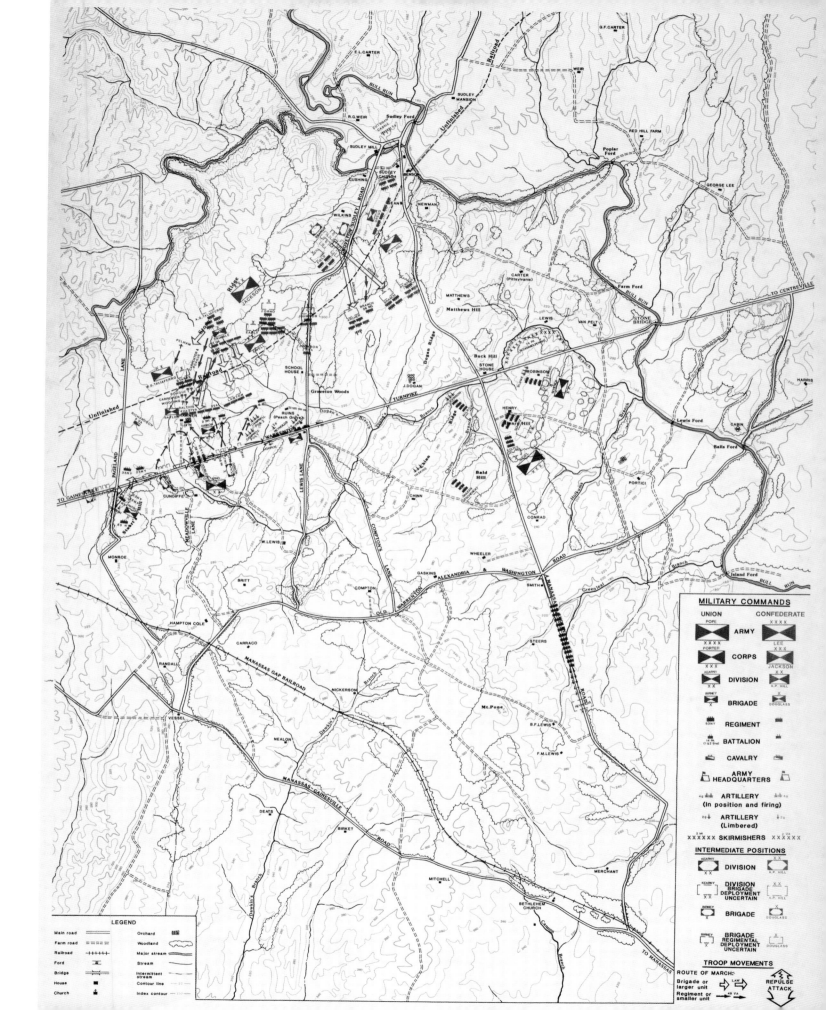

BULL RUN

RAILROAD

E.L. CARTER

G.F. CARTER

SUDLEY
MANSION

WEIR

RED HILL FARM

R.G. WEIR

POPLAR
FORD

SUDLEY FORD

SUDLEY MILL

GEORGE LEE

CUSHING

SUDLEY
CHURCH

BENSON

Unfinished

WILKINS

MCLEAN

NEWMAN

CARTER
(Pittsylvania)

Farm Ford

Bull Run

TO CENTREVILLE

Ridge

JACKSON

A.G. TALIAFERRO

EARLY

BELL

MATTHEWS

Matthews Hill

BRANCH

LEWIS

VAN PELT

STONE
BRIDGE

PELHAM

COMPTON

Buck Hill

STONE
HOUSE

ROBINSON

SCHOOL
HOUSE

J. DOGAN

Dogan Ridge

TURNPIKE

HARRIS

B. TALIAFERRO

Railroad

Unfinished

RUINS
(Peach Grove)

Dogan's

Branch

HENRY

Henry Hill

Lewis Ford

CABIN

BALLS FORD

RICHARDSON

BALDWIN-TURNER

WARRENTON

L. Lewis

Chinn Ridge

PORTICI

TO GAINESVILLE

35 NY 35 NY

Bald
Hill

CUNDIFF

CHINN

PAGELAND LANE

MEADOWVILLE
LANE

W. LEWIS

Young's Branch

LEWIS LANE

COMPTON'S LANE

CONRAD

Island Ford

BULL RUN

MONROE

BRITT

WHEELER

ALEXANDRIA &

WASHINGTON

ROAD

Greenleaf

Branch

HAMPTON COLE

COMPTON

GASKINS

SMITH

MANASSAS

CARRACO

OLD

WARRENTON

STEERS

RANDALL

MANASSAS GAP RAILROAD

NICKERSON

Branch

Mt. Pope

ROAD

VESSEL

NEALON

Dawkin's

B.F. LEWIS

MANASSAS-GAINESVILLE

F.M. LEWIS

DEATS

BIRKET

ROAD

MITCHELL

MERCHANT

Dawkin's Branch

BETHLEHEM
CHURCH

Cannon

Branch

TO MANASSAS

at what became known as Second Manassas (or Second Bull Run) came as something of a surprise to many observers, including several members of the president's cabinet, who advised against the move. But Lincoln had his reasons. "We must use the tools we have," he observed. "There is no man in the Army who can man these fortifications and lick these troops into shape half as well as he. If he can't fight himself, he excels in making others ready to fight." Within days McClellan was on the move west to engage Lee. Before long he benefited from a stroke of good fortune when his men came across a copy of Lee's operational plan to divide his army into five parts in order to capture Harpers Ferry. It looked as if McClellan might have the opportunity to deliver a crushing blow against Lee's scattered forces. The location for the confrontation was to be Antietam Creek near Sharpsburg, Maryland.

The Second Battle of Bull Run on August 29–30, 1862, was a much larger affair than the engagement a year earlier, but as with the previous battle, the result was a Union defeat.

The Battle of Antietam
September 16–18, 1862

THE CARNAGE AT ANTIETAM, the bloodiest single day of command in the entire war, shocked soldiers who walked across the field once the fighting had ceased. The battle suggested that the quest for a decisive triumph in climactic combat would be thwarted absent exceptional circumstances. Lee had placed his army in a precarious position, escaping disaster when McClellan proved unable to exploit his opportunities. Lee's failures north of the Potomac would balance his string of victories south of that river through the end of 1863.

Lee quickly realized that McClellan was aware of his plan, but nevertheless decided to carry it out, hoping that portions of his army could hold McClellan in check long enough for the remainder of his command to take Harpers Ferry. He succeeded: by the time McClellan finally pushed through, Confederate forces defending key passes across South Mountain on September 14, Stonewall Jackson had nearly surrounded the Union garrison at Harpers Ferry, securing its surrender the next day, with some 12,500 men becoming prisoners of war. Lee opted to stand and fight outside Sharpsburg, Maryland, deploying much of his command behind Antietam Creek east of the hamlet. McClellan declined to risk battle on September 16, preferring to await the arrival of more men before launching what he believed would be a crushing attack on September 17.

Although McClellan delivered telling blows in turn against the Confederate left and center, he could not coordinate his attacks, allowing Lee to scramble to preserve his position. An effort to crack the Confederate right was temporarily stymied when the Confederates thwarted attempts to ford Antietam Creek and to cross a stone bridge; by the time forces under Ambrose Burnside fought their way across the creek,

KEY FACTS: THE BATTLE OF ANTIETAM, SEPTEMBER 16–18 1862 RESULT: DRAW		
	Union	*Confederacy*
Units involved	Army of the Potomac	Army of Northern Virginia
Commanders	George B. McClellan	Robert E. Lee
Total Forces	87,000	45,000
Casualties	12,401	10,316

their attack on the Confederate right south of Sharpsburg was stopped cold by the arrival of Confederate reinforcements fresh from Harpers Ferry. As darkness came, the Confederates had held on. The next day Lee stood firm, daring McClellan to renew his challenge, and, when nothing happened, he vacated his lines, marching southward and recrossing the Potomac at Shepherdstown, Virginia, where his men checked McClellan's half-hearted pursuit.

Although initially Lee considered renewing his invasion of Maryland, he eventually rested content with defending northern Virginia while McClellan rested and refitted his command. The operation had failed to rouse support for the Confederacy in central and western Maryland, where it was never strong, and the withdrawal southward dashed hopes that somehow England or France (or both) would intervene in the wake of another Confederate triumph.

Casualties on the battlefield at Antietam. The 17 September engagement resulted in the most deadly day in American military history.

What was in fact a draw on the battlefield at Antietam appeared to resemble a defeat after Lee's retreat, presenting Lincoln with the opportunity to release his proclamation of emancipation. On September 22 the president did just that. He gave Confederates 100 days to return to the Union or face the legal end of slavery in areas still under Confederate control. Either the conflict would end or it would be transformed.

Although blacks and those Republicans who had pushed hard for emancipation welcomed the news of Lincoln's proclamation as signifying progress in the struggle against slavery, it alienated many Northern Democrats who endorsed a war to restore the republic so long as it did not strike at slavery. Confederates pointed to the proclamation as revealing what they had argued all along: that Lincoln meant to destroy the Southern way of life and incite insurrection among the slaves by promising them freedom. Far from weakening Confederate morale, the proclamation intensified it, at least in the short term. Responding to the possibility of uprisings among slaves, the Confederate Congress modified its conscription legislation to exempt one white adult male for anyone who owned 20 or more slaves. Although the measure's intention was to provide for greater security against black violence, it angered white

At the Battle of Corinth on October 3–4, 1862, Confederate forces sought control of the crucial rail junction at the town which had been captured by the Union that spring.

Southerners who owned less than 20 slaves or none at all. Was this going to be a rich man's war but a poor man's fight? Finally, the announcement of the preliminary proclamation, while it was endorsed by many antislavery Europeans, especially in Great Britain, did not entirely quell talk of intervention. Instead, some pro-Confederate Englishmen actually used the news of the forthcoming proclamation to argue for the necessity of intervention on supposedly humanitarian grounds to prevent the chaos, disorder, and violence of possible slave uprisings. This position proved less than persuasive, but it soon became clear that the promise of emancipation meant not just an escalation of the conflict but also its prolongation.

The end of Lee's Maryland campaign did not mean the end of Confederate efforts to deal a telling blow in advance of the midterm elections throughout the North. In Kentucky the Confederate drive to reclaim the state enjoyed sufficient initial success to see the installation of a Confederate governor, but when Don Carlos Buell's Army of the Ohio clashed with Braxton Bragg's Army of Tennessee at Perryville, Kentucky, on October 8, the Confederates declined to take advantage of a narrow tactical victory and retreated southward, effectively abandoning attempts to turn Kentucky Confederate. On the Tennessee–Mississippi border, although Ulysses S. Grant failed to follow up an opportunity to destroy a Confederate force at Iuka, Mississippi, on September 19, the Confederates in turn were unable to defeat part of Grant's army under William S. Rosecrans at Corinth, Mississippi, on October 3–4.

An opportunity that had looked so promising for the Confederacy in August had resulted in disappointment by October. Yet prospects seemed no brighter for the Union. Democrats denounced Lincoln's emancipation proclamation as a tyrannical measure that meant that white men would be forced to shed their blood so that black people would be free, a price that white prejudice found unacceptable. Lincoln's measures to punish disloyalty, which to some people looked remarkably

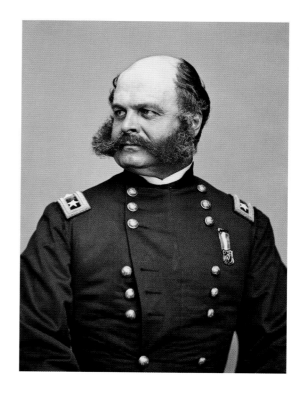

like efforts to quell dissent and undermine opposition, only added to the Democratic charge that the war to save the republic was overthrowing it. In the midterm elections Democrats eroded Republican margins in both houses of Congress, as well as wresting away several state legislatures and governorships from Republicans.

In the wake of these setbacks, a defiant Lincoln removed from command two generals deemed as conservative in their politics as they were cautious on the battlefield. Don Carlos Buell gave way to William S. Rosecrans in late October as head of what Rosecrans would soon call the Army of the Cumberland, while at long last George B. McClellan lost his beloved Army of the Potomac to Ambrose Burnside. Linked with the dismissal from the service of one of McClellan's staff officers for disloyalty and the court-martial of favored McClellan corps commander Fitz-John Porter for his performance at Second Manassas, it looked as if the president was demanding enthusiastic adherence to administration policies favoring a vigorous prosecution of the war, including confiscation and emancipation, as well as success on the battlefield.

A print of the Emancipation Proclamation from 1863. By this time, Lincoln was able to present the abolition of slavery as both a moral duty and a military necessity.

Emancipation Proclaimed

Having announced his willingness to embrace emancipation as a war aim essential to the achieving of Union victory, Lincoln nevertheless sought one last time to build support for his preferred approach to ending slavery. He made his case in his second annual message, issued as Congress convened in December 1862. After outlining once more his preference for gradual emancipation featuring compensation for masters and the voluntary relocation of the emancipated, he raised the rhetorical stakes. "The dogmas of the quiet past, are inadequate to the stormy present," he declared. "The occasion is piled high with difficulty, and we must rise—with the occasion. As our case is new, so we must think anew, and act anew." Once Lincoln had argued that his plan was a conservative measure designed to prevent revolutionary upheaval; now he claimed that it was a new way to deal with an old problem. "Fellow-citizens, we cannot escape history," he reminded Americans. "We of this Congress and this administration, will be remembered in spite of ourselves." It was time to act: "In giving freedom to the slave, we assure freedom to the free—honorable alike in what we give, and what we preserve. We shall nobly save, or meanly lose, the last best hope of earth. Other means may succeed; this could not fail."

Powerful words, these; but they fell on deaf ears. Slaveholders steadfastly refused to sell their slaves, believing that their labor would produce profits which far outpaced the price of their freedom. Free and freed African Americans showed little interest in leaving their American homeland, while the enslaved remained interested primarily in their eventual liberation. Lincoln's most prized legislative initiative simply wouldn't take with the very people who had to embrace it. Nor did Confederates race to re-enter the Union, choosing instead to support the quest for Southern independence.

Military affairs in December encouraged Confederate optimism. Ambrose Burnside looked to move quickly and cross the Rappahannock River at Fredericksburg, Virginia, before challenging Robert E. Lee to a footrace for Richmond. However, the equipment necessary to build pontoon bridges failed to appear in timely fashion, and Burnside decided to wait for its arrival, allowing Lee to occupy Fredericksburg. When Confederates blocked Burnside's efforts to bridge the river on December 11, he forced a crossing, in part by bombarding Fredericksburg itself. Two days later, on December 13, he attacked Lee's army west of town, but suffered ignominious defeat at great cost. Burnside withdrew his battered command across the river, leaving Lee to reflect that what looked to be a decisive victory was nevertheless incomplete, for the Army of the Potomac remained prepared to fight another day. Lincoln came to the same realization. Horrible as it might seem, if a Fredericksburg was fought every week, the "awful arithmetic" of attrition would eventually destroy Lee's army. Whether the tremendous losses that would guarantee such a result could be tolerated by the Northern public was altogether a different matter.

General Rosecrans at the Battle of Murfreesboro, December 31, 1862. Rosecrans claimed victory, but the reality was less clear cut.

To the west, in the Mississippi Valley, Union forces suffered another setback as the year came to an end, when Ulysses S. Grant's initial effort to capture Vicksburg, the Confederacy's strongest remaining citadel along the river, collapsed as cavalry raids severed Grant's supply lines while William T. Sherman failed to overcome Confederate fortifications north of the city. Matters were little better in central Tennessee as 1862 came to an end. At Murfreesboro, southeast of Nashville, Bragg's Army of Tennessee attacked Rosecrans's Army of the Cumberland on New Year's Eve; two days later, after failing to break the Yankees, Bragg withdrew, with both sides claiming victory in what passed for a slim cause for optimism in the North.

Even as Bragg planned his final attack against Rosecrans, however, the time had come for Lincoln to act upon his pledge to strike against slavery. January 1, 1863, marked the end of his hundred days of waiting. After a day of shaking hands, the president sat down and signed the Emancipation Proclamation. He had exhausted all alternatives, and the war to save the Union now accepted that striking at slavery, not leaving it alone, was essential to achieving that goal. The proclamation specified where the legality of slavery would no longer be recognized by the United States: in most cases this was territory held by the Confederacy, but there were areas where emancipation was immediate, and all of Tennessee was excluded from the document's coverage at the request of the state's military governor, Andrew Johnson. While the proclamation warned against slave rebellion, it opened the door to the widespread enlistment of African Americans as soldiers, which would prove a powerful blow.

By the end of 1862 a war to save the republic was promising to transform it. The shape of that transformation would depend upon the course the conflict took in the years to come.

The Battle of Fredericksburg, December 11–15, 1862, was one of the most uneven battles of the war, seeing more than twice as many Union soldiers killed as Confederates.

The Battle of Gettysburg in July 1863 saw the deaths of more than 50,000 soldiers in the costliest battle of the Civil War.

CHAPTER 5
TRIUMPH IN THE WEST, STALEMATE IN THE EAST

The Emancipation Proclamation transformed the American Civil War from a struggle to preserve an old order into a conflict that would transform both adversaries. Gone was the idea of a limited war fought in measured ways to enhance the chances of a rapid reconciliation between whites. With emancipation came the mobilization of former slaves and free blacks as combat soldiers for United States forces. Still, Confederate forces stood firm as the year 1863 opened, having halted Union advances during the winter: Confederate soldiers and leaders possessed redoubled determination now that the destruction of slavery was an avowed war aim of the enemy.

By year's end, however, it would be the Union which had achieved significant victories that divided the Confederacy, opened the door to an invasion of the Confederate heartland, and kept Robert E. Lee's Army of Northern Virginia in check in Virginia. Coastal operations, especially off Charleston, South Carolina, had tightened the blockade. Most importantly, victories at Vicksburg and Chattanooga had advanced Ulysses S. Grant to the forefront of Union military leadership as a general who got the job done.

Vicksburg: Persistence Pays Off

At the end of January 1863, Ulysses S. Grant took charge of operations against Vicksburg, the Confederacy's most important remaining military stronghold along the Mississippi. His Army of the Tennessee was posted on the west bank of the river, opposite the city, with some forces holding Memphis, Tennessee. The problem before Grant was simple to understand but difficult to solve: how could he transfer his forces across the Mississippi to launch an attack on the Confederate fortress? The city itself stood high on a bluff along the east bank; to the north the Yazoo River bordered an extensive delta area that was nearly impenetrable, while Grant would have to run transports by Vicksburg's batteries if he were to approach the city via a river crossing to the south. It might be worth the trouble of digging a canal to divert the flow of the Mississippi so that Union forces might advance against it, but such an endeavor would be time-consuming with uncertain results. Grant immediately rejected another option: to return to Memphis and attempt another overland drive. To do that in the wake of several Union setbacks would look too much like a confession of defeat followed by an inglorious retreat that might cost Grant his command, especially given ambitious subordinate John McClernand's continuing carping criticism of Grant in correspondence with President Lincoln.

For some ten weeks Grant explored his options, but the wet ground, cold weather, and the challenges posed by an unyielding and tenacious terrain thwarted various expeditions and projects, including several efforts at digging canals to divert the river. Northern media and some of his own generals, led by McClernand, prophesied failure as they sought Grant's removal. They argued that Grant was an incompetent and unimaginative drunk who was overmatched by the task before him, and they pointed to evidence of unhappiness about emancipation and the enlistment of black soldiers among some of his subordinates as proof that Grant could not be trusted to carry out the policies of the Lincoln administration. As spring came Lincoln was sufficiently anxious to dispatch several envoys west, ostensibly to oversee administrative matters, but in truth to find out whether the rumors circulating about Grant were true and justified replacing him.

These envoys arrived just as Grant was ready to take advantage of the advent of spring, with warmer temperatures and drying ground, to launch an ambitious operation. Gunboats and transports under the command of acting Rear Admiral David D. Porter would have to run past the Vicksburg batteries at night, then meet Grant's forces as they marched southward and ferry them across the Mississippi below Vicksburg. Once on dry land east of the river, Grant planned to move across central Mississippi, setting aside directives from Washington that preferred he join forces with Nathaniel P. Banks's Army of the Gulf in northern Louisiana. To divert the attention of Vicksburg's commander, John C. Pemberton, Grant instructed William T. Sherman to remain west of Vicksburg and act as if he was readying another offensive north of the city, while a column of Union cavalry under the command of Colonel Benjamin Grierson departed from southern Tennessee southward on a raid across the state of Mississippi, thus confusing Pemberton as to Union intentions.

The plan worked. Union gunboats and transports survived the gauntlet of artillery fire at Vicksburg in mid-April; by the end of the month, they were assisting Grant to cross the Mississippi and advance northward against scattered Confederate forces while Pemberton struggled to

The Union gunboats under the command of Admiral Porter run the blockade at Vicksburg on April 16, 1863.

The assault on Vicksburg by Union troops on July 4, 1863. The siege lasted for more than 40 days and two previous attempts to take the fort had failed before Grant finally succeeded.

discern enemy intentions. Once Grant defeated a Confederate force at Port Gibson and secured a base of operations at Grand Gulf, he called upon Sherman to join him before advancing against Vicksburg via the state capital at Jackson, some 45 miles due east of Vicksburg, where he could destroy railroads that might have helped the Confederates gather to counterattack. He decided to have his men live off the produce of the countryside, with wagon convoys bringing up ammunition, medical supplies, and other essentials. Within a week he defeated the Confederates at Raymond, Jackson, and Champion Hill, forcing Pemberton back into Vicksburg by May 18. Two attempts to take the Vicksburg fortifications by assault failed, and Grant settled down to lay siege to the city, re-establishing his supply line and gathering reinforcements to guard against a Confederate effort to rescue the beleaguered garrison. He also took advantage of a misstep by McClernand to secure the removal of his rival from command, secure in his knowledge that the president did not displace victorious generals.

Lincoln watched Grant's progress and set aside his reservations about the general. "He doesn't worry and bother me," he explained. "He isn't shrieking for reinforcements all the time…. And if Grant only does this thing down there—I don't care much how, so long as he does it right—why, Grant is my man and I am his the rest of the war!"

Chancellorsville: The Cost of Victory

Even as Grant commenced his spring offensive against Vicksburg, the Army of the Potomac, under yet another new commander, prepared to move south once more to meet Robert E. Lee and the Army of Northern Virginia. Joseph Hooker replaced Ambrose Burnside in January 1863 after it became evident that Burnside no longer

Joseph Hooker was appointed as commander of the Army of the Potomac in January 1863.

possessed the confidence of several of his generals after Fredericksburg and a January operation that literally got bogged down in the mud. Hooker was brash and confident to the point that he believed that what the nation most needed was a dictator to take charge. Lincoln quickly admonished him: "Only those generals who gain successes can set up dictators. What I now ask of you is military success, and I will risk the dictatorship.... Beware of rashness, but with energy, and sleepless vigilance, go forward, and give us victories." The man that people had dubbed "Fighting Joe" proposed to do just that, after doing what he could to rebuild the morale of his army in the wake of the Fredericksburg debacle. He would not move until spring.

South of the Rapidan and Rappahannock rivers, Robert E. Lee waited, his army weakened by the detachment of several divisions southward to gather supplies and hold Union coastal operations in check. That detachment plus Hooker's ability to amass numbers meant that the Federals had twice as many men as Lee did (the Army of the Potomac was never larger than it was on the eve of Hooker's offensive). Lee's victory at Fredericksburg might have prevented a Union advance, but it did little other than depress Union morale, and Lee still

lusted after a decisive victory that might turn the tide of the war. Hooker, however, believed he had the ideal opportunity to crush Lee. Dividing his army and leaving a significant portion opposite Fredericksburg, he proposed to sweep around Lee's left, cross the Rapidan and Rappahannock river line, and trap Lee between his two columns while Yankee cavalry continued southward to cut the Confederates off from Richmond.

Hooker commenced advancing during the last week of April at the same time Grant was making his way south of Vicksburg. Lee offered little opposition, and by May 1 Hooker had crossed the rivers, with his right wing bearing down on the Confederates. However, he decided not to press his advantage, and deployed his forces around a crossroads tavern known as Chancellorsville. Lee, having left about 10,000 men to keep an eye on the Federals in the Fredericksburg area, conferred with Stonewall Jackson about using the thickly wooded area to conceal a Confederate counterstrike against the extreme right of Hooker's army. Jackson proposed to take his entire command on what would be a time-consuming march to get into position: Lee would have to spend most of May 2 pinning Hooker in place with far fewer men. When Hooker did not press his advantage aggressively, Lee and Jackson sprung their trap, with Jackson's men rolling over the Union lines west of Chancellorsville. However, it was not until late afternoon that Jackson was in position, and as dusk fell he attempted to press his advantage, only to be felled by a volley fired by his own troops. The next day the Confederates forced Hooker to abandon his position around Chancellorsville while delaying a Federal thrust westward from Fredericksburg; the following day they checked and turned back that threat before focusing once more on Hooker. Just as Lee prepared to deliver one final blow against Hooker, the Union commander abandoned his well-fortified position—one Lee might have found difficult to take—and retreated north of the river line.

Once more Lee claimed complete triumph on the battlefield, although this time at a far

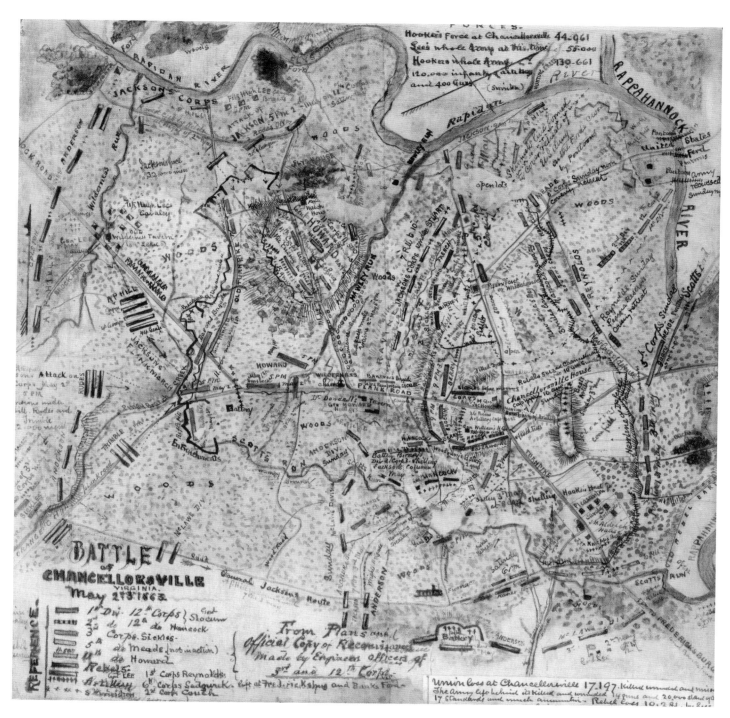

A map of the Battle of Chancellorsville, May 2–3, 1863, showing the various positions of the Union and Confederate forces over the course of the battle.

more significant cost than at Fredericksburg. Losing just under 13,000 men (out of just over 60,000 men available) was bad enough, but Jackson succumbed to his wounds and died on May 10. Hooker suffered over 17,000 casualties in a force nearly 134,000 strong, but what hit his army equally hard was the termination of the enlistments of soldiers who had signed up for two years in 1861. For all the tactical brilliance and audacity Lee had displayed, the end result simply prolonged the strategic stalemate in Virginia at a far higher cost than Fredericksburg. How, he pondered, could he strike the blow that would bring the Union to its knees?

The Battle of Gettysburg
July 1–3, 1863

Hungry for a decisive victory that would impact beyond the battlefield, Lee travelled to Richmond to discuss Confederate options with Jefferson Davis and his advisers days after his victory at Chancellorsville in May 1863. Davis, a Mississippian, was concerned about checking General Grant in his home state, but Lee maintained that the best response was to launch an invasion northward across the Potomac. Such a move would allow Virginia farmers to gather a crop while Lee's men foraged off Northern resources; the presence of Confederate armies in Union territory might well foster more criticism of the Lincoln administration, and might even revive talk of European intervention. Lee hoped for even more. He shared with one of his division commanders his belief that "our army would be invincible if it could be properly organized and officered. There never were such men in an army before. They will go anywhere and do anything if properly led." Now that Jackson was gone, changes had to be made, but in the aftermath of two Union defeats opportunity beckoned. Might not Lee finally have the chance to deliver the blow he had long imagined?

By June, Lee was ready, his army reunited, with two new corps commanders, A. P. Hill and Richard S. Ewell, both of whom had garnered plaudits for their skill as division commanders, joining senior corps commander James Longstreet and cavalry commander Jeb Stuart. They moved northward through the Shenandoah Valley, crossed the Potomac, and this time left Maryland behind as they entered south-central Pennsylvania. Ahead

lay the state capitol at Harrisburg behind the Susquehanna River; beyond that more railroads, coal mines, and factories awaited, the loss of which would deal a severe blow to Union resources. Lee's men stripped the countryside of what they could and acted under orders to capture African Americans in the area with the intention of determining whether they were fugitive slaves to

Meade took command of the Army of the Potomac after Hooker's resignation on June 28, 1863.

KEY FACTS:
THE BATTLE OF GETTYSBURG, JULY 1–3, 1863
RESULT: UNION VICTORY

	Union	Confederacy
Units involved	Army of the Potomac	Army of Northern Virginia
Commanders	George G. Meade	Robert E. Lee
Total Forces	93,921	71,699
Casualties	23,049	28,063

be returned south. Receiving orders to swing once more around the Army of the Potomac, Stuart launched another of his raids, hoping to regain some of the glory he had lost when Union cavalry had handled his troopers roughly at the outset of the campaign at Brandy Station.

Hooker shifted his army northward, shielding Washington from the invaders while looking for an opportunity to strike. It did not help that many of his subordinates complained about him as he had once complained about McClellan and Burnside, or that Lincoln entertained these complaints much as he had those about McClellan, Burnside, and Grant. Offended that he did not get his way when he requested that the garrison at Harpers Ferry be placed under his command, Hooker offered his resignation, which Lincoln quickly accepted. The army's new commander was George G. Meade, a grizzled general who had tried with mixed success to avoid the political whirl that surrounded the Army of the Potomac.

Learning of Meade's elevation to command, Lee knew little else, because Union forces kept blocking Stuart's path back to Lee's army, depriving Lee of Stuart's abilities to reconnoiter and gather information. Lee decided to bring his army together, knowing full well that to do so would virtually guarantee that a battle would be fought somewhere soon, because a large concentrated army could not survive by foraging for long. Meanwhile, Meade prepared a defensive

position in northern Maryland while sending forces ahead to keep an eye on Lee. Between the two armies was the crossroads town of Gettysburg, with a road network that drew both armies toward the county seat of Adams County. On July 1 Confederate infantry encountered Union cavalry north and west of the town, with reinforcements on both sides soon making their way to the field. It was a battle no one wanted, but now it seemed impossible to avoid. Was this the chance, however less than ideal, that Lee sought—especially with Meade new to his responsibilities?

By the afternoon of July 1, the Confederates, taking advantage of a road network favorable to the rather quick concentration of their command, had driven the Union defenders through the town to an array of hills south of it. Under orders from Lee to continue the attack "if practicable" but "to avoid a general engagement" until the rest of the army was up, Richard Ewell decided to await reinforcements and give his men a much-needed rest after hours of marching and fighting under a summer sun; by the time reinforcements came, the Union position, already challenging, had solidified. During the night men from both sides made their way to Gettysburg; Stuart and his horsemen would not arrive until late the next day.

Although Longstreet, with visions of Fredericksburg fresh in his mind, advised taking up a defensive position to force Meade to attack, Lee decided to press his advantage, aiming to replicate

BATTLE of GETTYSBURG Penna

Showing Positions held 1st and 3rd JULY. 1863.

from Official Map of US Engineers. July 1863.

234
No 286

Reference.

Union Forces
Rebel Forces
Artillery
Sharpshooters
Houses

97.105 287 guns
Cavalry 210-192
Roads

A map of the Battle of Gettysburg, showing the arrangement of Union and Confederate forces through the course of the engagement.

Major General Winfield S. Hancock rides behind Union lines as they prepared to defend against Pickett's Charge on the final day of the battle, July 3, 1863.

his achievement at Chancellorsville. On the morning of July 2, he ordered Longstreet to take two divisions on a march through wooded areas to conceal them from sight as they made their way to attack the seemingly vulnerable Union left flank. As at Chancellorsville, it would take time for Longstreet to get into position, especially when he had to countermarch upon discovering that the original line of march was vulnerable to discovery by enemy units deployed on a rock-strewn hill later known as Little Round Top. Nor did it help that, as time passed, more Union forces arrived, while corps commander Daniel E. Sickles advanced his

command westward from the main Union line, only to stretch it too thin as he took up a problematic line of defense. If Lee held Meade in high regard, as some postwar recollections suggested, he did not show it on this day, apparently expecting the situation to remain static as his men took their places. As they deployed on the afternoon of July 2, they unexpectedly came under fire from soldiers who were where they were not supposed to be in the minds of either army commander.

Over the next several hours, Longstreet's two divisions, joined by one of A. P. Hill's divisions, launched a massive assault across farmland,

woods, and hills that seemed at times on the verge of success. Although Sickles's men put up a fight, their position was untenable, and as their commander fell wounded they pulled back. Union reinforcements rushed forward to secure Little Round Top and a slope known as Cemetery Ridge, where the center of Meade's line rested, sometimes in the nick of time. Meade hurried reinforcements from his right to bolster his defense, leaving his left, holding a brace of hills (Cemetery and Culp's Hills) just south of Gettysburg, vulnerable to a late afternoon attack by Ewell's divisions that threatened to get into the Union rear and sever its lines of communication along the Baltimore Pike. Once more Union forces held on; if they had been bent, they had not broken.

This photograph of the casualties at the Battle of Gettysburg by Timothy O'Sullivan, entitled A Harvest of Death, *became one of the iconic images of the horrors of the Civil War.*

Union left flank. Lee then settled upon an attack by three divisions with infantry and artillery support against the Union center, arrayed along the northern portion of Cemetery Ridge, with the recently arrived Stuart sent to engage Union forces due east of Gettysburg.

The ensuing assault, taking place in the early afternoon of July 3 after Confederate artillery bombarded the Union line, proved to be a stirring spectacle that ended in bloody and abject failure. It was Fredericksburg, but in reverse. Stuart's sally was no more successful. Meade contemplated but decided against a counterattack, and after rain drenched both sides on July 4, Lee commenced a withdrawal, hoping to recross the Potomac and return to Virginia. Meade pursued, although not as vigorously as some people, including Lincoln, wished, and fell short of bringing Lee to battle once more north of the Potomac.

Although Lee's expedition had served to improve Confederate logistics, including his food supply, it kept the war out of Virginia for barely a month. Moreover, his tremendous losses (some 28,000 men out of perhaps 72,000 engaged) cost him manpower he would sorely need the next year (Meade lost some 23,000 men out of approximately 90,000 engaged). He had not broken Union morale or encouraged foreign intervention, and he had not broken the strategic stalemate that continued to exist in the eastern theater. Nor had his campaign had any impact on Grant's operations against Vicksburg. At about the same hour as the July 3 assault ended in disaster to the west, Grant and Pemberton met between the lines to discuss the terms of Confederate capitulation. The following day, Vicksburg surrendered, with some 30,000 Confederate soldiers taken prisoner and paroled in the hope that they would return home and share their discouragement with Confederate civilians. Grant had achieved the triumph Lee had sought. Within a week another Confederate surrender at Port Hudson, Louisiana, secured control of the Mississippi River for the United States, thus driving a wedge through the Confederacy.

That night Meade met with his commanders and decided to stay put and await Lee's next move. At first Lee wanted to renew the offensive against the flanks, only to be thwarted when fighting opened before dawn at Culp's Hill, with Union forces driving the Confederates away, while Longstreet's men were in no position to renew their advance against a much stronger

Tullahoma, Chickamauga, Chattanooga

While Grant and Hooker took the offensive in the spring of 1863, William S. Rosecrans did not direct his Army of the Cumberland to advance against Braxton Bragg's Army of Tennessee in central Tennessee. He complained he was not ready and would not be hurried into premature combat. When he began to move in the last week of June, however, he quickly outmaneuvered Bragg, driving the Confederates south toward Chattanooga without fighting a pitched battle. Some six weeks later Rosecrans resumed his advance, once more outflanking Bragg, who abandoned Chattanooga and retreated out of Tennessee into northern Georgia during the first week of September.

Having already rejected Robert E. Lee's offer to resign his command in the wake of the defeat

The respective generals of the Army of Tennessee and the Army of the Cumberland, Braxton Bragg (left) and William S. Rosecrans (right). Rosecrans bided his time and waited for the perfect moment to launch a devastating attack in June 1863.

at Gettysburg, Jefferson Davis implored him to go west and take over for Bragg. When Lee demurred, Davis did on September what he had failed to do in May, directing Lee to send forces west to bolster Bragg. Lee chose Longstreet for the assignment, and before long two divisions were on their way over the makeshift Confederate rail network to northern Georgia. Assured of

The Battle of Chickamauga lasted from September 18–20, 1863. The result was a stunning defeat for the Union forces.

reinforcements, Bragg decided that it was time to strike back at Rosecrans. Failing to hit a portion of Rosecrans's army before it had reunited, Bragg then made contact on September 18 and opened his assault the next day, just as Longstreet's men were arriving. The following day, taking advantage of some Yankee mishandling of defensive deployment, Longstreet's two divisions—the same two divisions that had hammered Sickles at Gettysburg—tore through the bluecoat line, sending Rosecrans and portions of his army reeling back toward Chattanooga. Only a determined defensive stand by George H. Thomas prevented complete disaster, earning Thomas the nickname "the Rock of Chickamauga." As evening fell Thomas deliberately pulled back toward Chattanooga, reaching it after dark on September 21. Bragg's victorious army followed, and before long draped themselves around the heights surrounding the city and commenced laying siege to it and its defenders. It was perhaps the greatest Confederate victory outside Virginia during the war.

Realizing Chattanooga's importance as the gateway to the Confederate heartland, Lincoln hurried reinforcements from Meade's Army of the Potomac and Grant's Army of the Tennessee to try to rescue Rosecrans. Reports reached Washington, however, that Rosecrans was so shaken by the defeat (Lincoln remarked that Rosecrans acted like a duck hit on the head, a rare sight in any case) that perhaps it would be best if someone else took over. Lincoln went one step further, naming Grant commander of virtually all forces from the Appalachian Mountains to the Mississippi River and allowing him to choose between Rosecrans and Thomas to head the Army of the Cumberland. Grant chose Thomas, then chose to come to Chattanooga to see what he could do. Arriving on October 23, he soon put into action a plan devised by Rosecrans and others to reopen a line of supply to Chattanooga and began readying the forces assembling there to take the offensive, all the while reading reminders from Lincoln to keep an eye upon Knoxville, where Ambrose Burnside was doing his best to retain control of the city despite rumored supply problems.

Grant's task at Chattanooga became easier when Bragg, struggling with contentious subordinates, dispatched a sullen Longstreet to attack Union forces occupying Knoxville, Tennessee. Perhaps he thought that his defensive line, anchored by Lookout Mountain to the south and the steep slopes of Missionary Ridge east of Chattanooga, could withstand anything Grant might do. He was wrong. In a series of attacks between November 23 and 25, forces under Grant's direction swept over Lookout Mountain and Missionary Ridge, dislodging the Confederates from positions deemed impenetrable. The Confederates retreated into northern Georgia, with Bragg losing his command, while Grant was now beyond doubt the Union's leading general.

A photograph of Lookout Mountain taken in 1864.

Toward 1864

There was fighting elsewhere too in 1863, from the evolving guerilla war in Kansas to operations along the south Atlantic seacoast, including several months of attacking Confederate defenses outside Charleston, South Carolina. Throughout the fall, Lee and Meade moved against each other in Virginia without significant result. The Union blockade became ever more effective, while Union advances deprived the Confederacy of desperately needed resources. It was also the year in which newly raised regiments of African Americans, free and freed, proved that black Americans would fight for their freedom, as actions at Milliken's Bend, Louisiana; Port Hudson, Louisiana; and Battery Wagner, South Carolina, revealed. As Grant told Lincoln, "By arming the negro we have added a powerful ally. They will make good soldiers and taking them from the enemy weaken him in the same proportion they strengthen us." Given that both Union and Confederate forces were suffering losses due to battle, desertion, and expiring enlistments, the issue of how to increase and preserve manpower was of critical importance.

Elections in 1863 saw the Republicans rebound from their losses in 1862. There was more optimism about the progress of Union arms after the victories of 1863, and the emergence of Grant suggested that at last the United States had found someone who could confront Robert E. Lee. For the Confederates, the loss of more men and territory and the defeat of the seemingly invincible Lee at Gettysburg was cause for uncertainty, yet there was also hope that a persistent defense might frustrate Union hopes and cause Lincoln to lose his bid for re-election. Thus the events of 1863, as dramatic as they were, were not decisive: both sides looked to 1864 as the critical year.

At the Battle of Missionary Ridge on November 25, 1863, the Union Army overcame fierce resistance and ended the siege of Chattanooga.

A recruiting poster for the United States Colored Troops from 1865.

A family at home in Cedar Mountain, Virginia, 1862.

CHAPTER 6
WAR AS REVOLUTION

Both the United States and the Confederacy went to war in 1861 to preserve something. But wars have a way of transforming the very things they are supposed to preserve, and at times may even destroy them. The war to preserve the Union changed it, as the government at Washington assumed new roles, wielded broader authority, and embraced measures that would have been hard to imagine in a previous time. It also may have accelerated institutional changes that would establish the framework for economic transformation, and it enabled Republicans to enact measures that would have been impossible to secure had Southerners remained in Congress.

Meanwhile, the founders of the Confederacy argued that they sought an independence they were willing to secure through war to preserve a way of life grounded in the institution of slavery, maintain a decentralized central government in the interest of preserving states' rights, and shield the Southern homeland from disruption. Yet the war challenged the institution of slavery and eroded it before destroying it altogether; it wreaked havoc with that cherished way of life;

it fostered a centralized government in Richmond that took necessary measures to wage war; and it disrupted and in some cases devastated the Southern homeland.

Mobilization

Neither side was ready in 1861 for the conflict that followed. While the Confederacy had already commenced raising an army of volunteers who enlisted for a year's service, Lincoln first called state militias into federal service, followed by enlistment calls for two-year and eventually three-year soldiers. At the same time, neither side possessed enough arms and supplies, although the Confederacy's seizure of United States armories helped make up for that situation. Both sides would import weapons, while in the North factories began turning out more rifles, revolvers, and artillery pieces. As the Confederacy possessed a single iron works at Richmond, it would depend on imports, seizures, and battlefield captures to secure cannon. Procurement procedures for arms, uniforms, and other material of war often lacked quality control, although as the war continued reliable suppliers were identified.

An 1861 Union print supporting volunteers for the Federal Army. When the war began, Lincoln called for 75,000 volunteers. It was not long before he realized the Union would need far more troops to defeat the Confederacy.

An incident from the New York Draft Riots of July 1863. The introduction of conscription led to protests across the country.

The United States Army at the beginning of the war represented but a handful of the men needed to subdue the Confederacy. Much of that force was deployed on the frontier west of the Mississippi, and a significant number of officers (although far fewer enlisted men) threw in their lot with the Confederacy. The United States volunteer forces, like their Confederate counterparts, drew from the civilian population and retired military men to form an officer corps; Lincoln also selected for generals' commissions men whose primary value lay in their supposed political clout or popular appeal, giving rise to the derisive term "political generals." Among them were Massachusetts Democrat Benjamin F. Butler, Massachusetts Republican Nathaniel P. Banks, and a number of officers with slight or no military experience who were trusted to rally immigrants to the colors, notably German Americans Franz Sigel and Carl Schurz and Irish American Thomas F. Meagher.

By 1862 volunteering in the North began to sag, aided by a mistaken decision to cease recruiting for a short period. In 1863 the United States decided to implement a system of conscription that called on Northern states to meet certain recruiting quotas (often sweetened by the inducement of financial rewards, known as bounties) or face conscription. Rarely was conscription triggered; nevertheless, it inspired resistance, in part because a drafted man could evade military service by either hiring a substitute or paying a commutation fee of $300. Protestors claimed that this meant that the rich and well-off could evade service. Moreover, some draftees had little interest in fighting in a war to free the slaves. The most famous of these protests was the New York City Draft Riots of 1863, in which mobs attacked recruiting stations, Republican newspapers, and black neighborhoods, churches, and an orphanage. Many conscripts sought to desert at the first opportunity, as did so-

called bounty jumpers, who enlisted, collected their bounties, deserted, and then enlisted elsewhere under a new name to secure another bounty. When the terms of the three-year volunteers were approaching their expiration date, federal and state recruiters offered a number of inducements, most of them financial, to secure reenlistment, but

only about half of the men eligible for discharge took advantage of the offer, while the remainder who survived combat left the service during the spring of 1864, creating a manpower strain that impaired Grant's strategic offensive based on applying superior resources systematically and simultaneously against the Confederacy.

Confederates who had volunteered for military service in 1861 did so for only a year. While many of these men reenlisted when the time came, others drifted homeward, having seen enough of war firsthand to suit them or eager to return home to provide for their family. But the Confederacy needed manpower, and so in April 1862 it resorted to conscription. As one might expect, the new policy incorporated exemptions, including various occupations that soon enjoyed popularity, and at one point provided for the purchase of a substitute, but most controversial was a decision made later that year to exempt one white male for every plantation with 20 or more slaves, with additional provisions for overseers working two nearby plantations with a total of 20 or more slaves.

To many white Southerners who either did not own any slaves or owned fewer than 20,

A Confederate soldier from Virginia in his volunteer uniform with his musket and bayonet.

The "Twenty Negro Law" allowed the wealthier portions of Southern society to escape military service.

The slaves named on this payroll worked on the Ashley Ferry Nitro Works in South Carolina. Rather than being paid themselves, the compensation for their labor went to their owners.

this exemption, commonly called the "Twenty Negro Law," was not so much a security or management measure as it was evidence that the larger slaveholders were escaping the obligation to serve to protect their own economic interests. In turn slaveholders complained about the practices of Confederate military authorities and eventually about legislation that provided for the impressment of slave labor into military service, suggesting that in time of war the status of slaves as private property was open to modification. Confederate armies needed enslaved labor to perform non-combat tasks, from erecting fortifications to supporting military operations by feeding soldiers and as wagon drivers.

These two acts struck at the heart of the Confederacy's identity. In a world where slaveholders insisted that they and non-slaveholders were united in a common cause, excluding whites managing significant numbers of slaves highlighted divisions along class lines, while those whites who owned fewer slaves found themselves stranded. For a government founded on the right of individuals to own human beings as private property to then compromise that property right by impressing slaves for military service led critics to wonder whether the Confederacy might be as much a threat to slavery as the Republican party, and tested slaveholders' loyalty to the new regime. The advancing United States forces, regardless of the inclinations of their commanders, became liberators, while the chaos of war offered enslaved people opportunities to escape to freedom.

Through 1863 both sides agreed to exchange prisoners captured during military operations. However, this system collapsed at the end of the year when the Confederates refused to exchange African American soldiers and failed to honor the terms of paroled prisoners from the capture of Vicksburg. Although he did not initiate the policy, Ulysses S. Grant upheld it, in part because it drained the Confederacy of manpower. Critics pointed to the horrid conditions of prisoners as justifying a more humane approach, but it was not until the Confederacy quietly decided to include African American prisoners in exchanges following the election of 1864 that the exchange system gradually resumed.

Soldiers on both sides deserted for various reasons. Some had taken enough of combat; some wanted to defraud the bounty system; some were needed at home. Yet Confederate forces could ill afford desertion, given their inferior manpower. Over time, of course, as hopes for Confederate victory crumbled and Union advances threatened Confederate homes, desertion increased in the Confederate army, with a significant portion of the Army of Northern Virginia melting away during the last week of the war.

Division, Dissent, and Disloyalty

Dissent at home is part of waging war. Whatever flush of unity appears when war breaks out soon dissipates, and people voice their disagreement with the conduct of military operations or wartime policies. Moreover, in the American Civil War, there were those who supported the goals of the other side. In the border states of Maryland, Kentucky, and Missouri, there were significant numbers of Confederate sympathizers who, if they had prevailed, would have taken their states into the new slaveholding republic. Meanwhile, in the Confederacy, white Unionists in Louisiana and in the Appalachian mountain chain remained loyal to the Union, especially in East Tennessee and parts of western Virginia and North Carolina. Enslaved people were far more interested in seeing the war as shaking the foundations of slavery and offering opportunities for autonomy and freedom, which most associated with Union victory. But the lines between dissent and disloyalty were not always obvious, and at times authorities on both sides cracked down hard on critics, activists, and people assisting the enemy.

At war's outset, with eastern Maryland filled with supporters of secession who were willing to assist the cause, Lincoln soon had to crack down on efforts to obstruct communications between Washington and the rest of the North, which ran through Baltimore. A mob attacked a Massachusetts regiment changing trains in Baltimore, and civilians engaged in acts of sabotage that a later generation might term domestic terrorism. With Congress not in session, Lincoln decided to suspend the privilege of the writ of habeas corpus to allow for the quick apprehension and imprisonment of such people. Acting in his capacity as district circuit court judge, Chief Justice Roger B. Taney contested Lincoln's act

The atrocious conditions at prison camps, like Andersonville in Georgia, shown here, made agreements on prisoner exchanges even more important.

of suspension in *Ex parte Merryman*, concerning the arrest of Marylander John Merryman for obstructing the movement of Union troops, but the federal government persisted. Over time Lincoln exercised his powers more broadly, despite Democratic complaints that he was becoming an unfettered tyrant; he defined discouraging enlistment as one act subject to arrest. Congress in 1863 authorized Lincoln to act, but provided that anyone arrested had to be tried, instead of being held without trial, otherwise they would be released. When in May 1863 Union authorities arrested Democrat Clement Vallandigham of Ohio for discouraging

enlistment, Lincoln avoided a court test that might make Vallandigham a martyr by releasing him into the hands of the Confederates (who did not know what to do with him) and then ignored Vallandigham when he returned north. The administration also authorized the arrest of newspaper editors who went too far in their opposition to the war, calling into question where one drew the line between disagreement, dissent, and disloyalty.

Northern Democrats divided over the policies of the Lincoln administration, with some supporting the war effort while others complained that the war to save the republic was destroying

Clement Vallandigham was arrested in 1863 for his anti-recruitment efforts. He soon attained national prominence as the leader of the Copperhead movement.

An 1864 cartoon from Harper's Weekly *satirizes the Copperheads' desire to make peace with the South.*

it by concentrating too much power in the hands of the federal government in general and the president in particular. These antiwar Democrats, called Copperheads, also opposed emancipation and would have been content to negotiate an end to the war that would have recognized Confederate independence; Vallandigham proved to be the most prominent member of this faction of the party. After 1862, many other Democrats, while still desirous of defeating the Confederacy, opposed the draft, emancipation, and the escalation of waging war beyond combat actions. They also denounced the ending of prisoner exchanges as abandoning Union prisoners of war to their fate. The Democratic appeal surged during times of Union military disaster and declined in the wake of Union victories: while they remained a minority during the war, they always posed a potent threat to the Lincoln administration.

Besides the divisions within Confederate ranks over conscription and impressment, the Davis administration had to address the persistence of white unionists in the South and governors who resented Richmond's intrusion into their affairs. For all that Confederate spokesmen had to say about the centrality of states' rights to their cause, when governors such as Georgia's Joseph E. Brown and North Carolina's Zebulon B. Vance disagreed with Davis over the treatment of their state's troops and conscription, the Confederate president became a proponent of national power. With the approval of the Confederate Congress, he also suspended the privilege of the writ of habeas corpus.

Both sides suffered from internal division, and both sides sought to stifle internal dissent, sometimes using harsh measures. Confiscation was controversial, period. Northern opposition to emancipation was matched by Southern anger over how the Confederacy treated slavery in its conscription and impressment policies. While these disputes hampered how both sides waged war, they did not determine the outcome, although the Confederacy could less afford divisions given their disadvantages elsewhere. Generals on both sides were mindful of the need to exacerbate such rifts and promote disaffection and disillusionment when planning military operations.

Finances and Legislation

Republicans' advocacy of state-fostered economic development became a reality, facilitated by the departure of Southern members of Congress that left them in a clear majority. Tariff legislation provided a source of revenue to support the war effort while it protected Northern manufacturing and other economic activity from foreign competition. Congress authorized the construction of a transcontinental railroad, passed legislation providing homesteads for whites moving westward, and established land-grant colleges. At the same time, however, it had to figure out how to pay for fighting a war.

The United States government chose to print its own money, increase taxes and create new ones, including an income tax, and borrow money through issuing bonds. Such actions would affect the nation's economic activity for decades to come. The Legal Tender Act of 1862 authorized the federal government to print its own currency to help keep economic activity going, although these so-called "greenbacks" were rarely worth their denomination in coins, with their worth declining

Though ostensibly strong advocates of states' rights, when it came to conflicts between governors, like Zebulon Vance of North Carolina pictured here, and Confederate President Jefferson Davis, they were always resolved in favor of the latter.

The first US dollar bill was introduced with the Legal Tender Act of 1862.

came to depend heavily on printing currency, which over time became subject to ever higher rates of inflation. If financing the war caused some discomfort to the United States, it inflicted major pain on a struggling Confederate economy that was already shrinking as the front line contracted. A decision to encourage planters not to ship cotton abroad in 1861 had limited effect given the surplus of cotton already in European warehouses; by the time the shortage began to be felt, cotton from other sources and from Union captures helped to meet demand, while the Confederacy missed the income it would normally have realized had it been able to secure export routes.

in accordance with dark days for the cause. The next year Congress passed legislation establishing federal banks and decided to tax state and local bank notes out of existence to establish a single national currency. With war's end came a struggle to reduce the inflated value of greenbacks by slowly withdrawing them from circulation while paying off war bonds, but the Union managed to make its way through the conflict in fairly good financial shape while skirting past some tight moments.

The Confederacy struggled to do nearly as well. Given the success of the United States blockade and the dearth of industry throughout the Confederacy, tariffs raised little money; so did excise taxes on exports, notably cotton. Direct taxation of goods and property (including slaves) proved only somewhat more successful, and Confederate bonds became a shaky proposition after military reverses in 1863. The Confederacy

Women's Changing Roles

With husbands and loved ones off at the front, white women on both sides were left to manage households, seek jobs, and support the war effort. Some did so by becoming nurses; others raised funds or made items for the troops. More working-class women entered manufacturing, while farmers' wives took over more responsibility to manage family farms as well as to share in the labor involved. For slaveholding families, women had to learn how to manage farms and plantation workforces without as many (if any) men, a situation that induced the Confederate government to provide for the presence of men in such situations through exemptions. Approximately 400 women even donned uniforms or shouldered a rifle, although they did their best to disguise their gender.

The Confederacy relied on printing currency to keep the war effort afloat.

In the North, women played major roles in sanitary fairs held to raise funds to help support the welfare of the men at the front. Many middle-class white women leaders such as Elizabeth Cady Stanton and Susan B. Anthony used women's support for the war effort to push for the enfranchisement of women; after the war they openly wondered why black men could be enfranchised while white women remained outside that central sphere of citizenship. Working-class women of both sides took to the streets to make their voices heard, especially during the Richmond Bread Riot of 1863, followed a few months later by the draft riots in New York City.

Much is made of the difference between battlefront and home front, but the ebb and flow of military operations turned home fronts into battlefronts and later into occupied territories in the case of Confederate women. This was an understandable cause of concern for Confederate soldiers who worried about the vulnerability of people at home. Moreover, as they had enlisted to defend home and hearth, what should they do now that home and hearth were under threat or even occupied? Was desertion to protect one's family truly dishonorable in such a situation?

Viewing War at Home

Civilians on both sides wanted to know what was going on at the front. They awaited news of battles and dreaded the accompanying casualty lists. Newspapers frequently offered misleading initial accounts of battles, and it often took a while to learn exactly what had happened, in part because war news was filtered through the

Elizabeth Cady Stanton and Susan B. Anthony were pioneers in the votes for women movement and they pointed to the work women were doing to support the war effort as evidence that they should be able to vote.

Matthew Brady's photographs provided civilians at home with hundreds of images of the war—and brought home to viewers the real horrors of war.

political preferences of the paper's editorial staff. At times letters from soldiers kept the folks at home informed of what the men were doing, and they returned the favor, keeping everyone up to date with events at home. Even as soldiers wanted news from home, they widely argued that no one not at the front could understand the experience of combat, and at times they complained that people at home needed to be more enthusiastic in support of the military effort.

Unable in most cases to travel to the front to see what war looked like, civilians looked to artists' renderings in weekly papers such at New York's *Harper's Weekly* to gain some idea of what a charge or a hospital looked like. Engravers such as Currier and Ives provided prints of battle scenes suitable for display on the wall. The increased popularity of photography offered yet another way to view war second-hand. Presidents, politicians, generals, and soldiers all posed for pictures; photographers offered camp scenes, terrain studies, battlefield sites, and that favorite image of dead bodies in a field. Chief among these photographers were Matthew Brady, Alexander Gardner, George N. Barnard, and Timothy O'Sullivan. No sooner had the smoke cleared from many a battlefield in Pennsylvania, Maryland, or Virginia than the photographers would rush in to secure their images. One reviewer of a Brady exhibition noted that the photographer "has done something to bring home to us the terrible reality and earnestness of war. If he has not brought bodies and laid them in our dooryards and along the streets, he has done something very like it." Yet the realism was limited: photographers moved bodies, posed in their own pictures, or photographed soldiers playing dead, while, given the technology of the period, there were no meaningful images of actual combat, merely its destructive aftermath.

Public anticipation of the outcome of military operations and their understanding of victory and defeat shaped support for the war effort and public assessment of the progress of military operations. Brought up on images of glorious battles such as Waterloo, civilians on both sides grew frustrated with the indecisiveness of battle. In 1864, for example, many Northerners anticipated that Grant would defeat Lee outright, and when that failed to happen, they did not see Grant's hold on Lee at Richmond and Petersburg as anything but a stalemate. However, they were inspired when Sherman took Atlanta, although military operations had already nullified the city's military importance; overlooked in the celebration was that John Bell Hood's army escaped to fight another day. Antietam became a victory due to Lee's withdrawal across the Potomac; Grant declined to return his forces to Memphis before approaching Vicksburg again because he knew that would look like a retreat and would thus place him at risk of losing his command. Generals were well aware of public perception and the need to dishearten civilian populations, while Grant and others learned that attempting to pacify and win over Confederate civilians in occupied territories rarely worked.

Blacks in Blue

The Emancipation Proclamation opened the way for African Americans to enlist in the armed forces of the United States in large numbers, exceeding initial attempts to arm them as soldiers in 1862. Free and freed black men often joined of their own accord, although Southern blacks were sometimes recruited in ways that suggested their enlistment was not altogether voluntary.

Critics of black enlistment openly questioned whether black recruits would fight. Over a six-week period in June and July 1863, black soldiers proved their critics wrong at Milliken's Bend, Louisiana; Port Hudson, Louisiana; and Battery Wagner outside Charleston, South Carolina. In each case black soldiers fought valiantly and fiercely, although for the remainder of 1863 most of them continued to serve in support roles rather than combat operations.

As for the Confederates, not only did they not recognize black Union soldiers as soldiers with the same status as their counterparts, but in several instances they slaughtered black soldiers rather than take them prisoner. The most infamous instance of this happened in April 1864 at Fort Pillow, Tennessee, north of Memphis on the Mississippi

River, when Confederate forces under cavalry commander Nathan Bedford Forrest, a prewar slave trader, overran the Union garrison and killed blacks attempting to surrender. Despite a previous pledge by the Lincoln administration to retaliate for such atrocities, there was no reprisal. The refusal of Confederate authorities to treat captured black Union soldiers as prisoners of war contributed to the collapse of the prisoner exchange system: how could Union authorities ask African Americans to fight for their freedom if they would not protect them from re-enslavement or death?

By 1864 African Americans were a critical part of the Union army, with one out of every seven soldiers serving in a black regiment. Black soldiers had battled for equal pay and equal treatment; they now formed a key part of the forces under Grant's overall command.

Yet black military service in the Union army slammed one door as it opened another. One could not continue to advocate colonization as a preferred policy if one was asking people to fight for a country they then must leave. Lincoln realized this, and although some scholars continue to suggest that the president's interest in colonization continued, he

no longer made it the centerpiece of his approach to ending slavery. Military service also opened the way to citizenship, as Frederick Douglass realized: "Once let the black man get upon his person the brass letter, U.S., let him get an eagle on his button, and a musket on his shoulder and bullets in his pocket, there is no power on earth that can deny that he has earned the right to citizenship." Ulysses S. Grant agreed, arguing that the road from laborer to soldier to citizen to voter was now open for black men as they moved forward.

The sight of armed black men in uniform was a sign of just how revolutionary the war had become. Women in the North would cite their patriotic activities as exhibitions of citizenship that in turn entitled them to vote; the United States Congress passed economic legislation that fundamentally shifted American economic development, while the destruction of slavery devastated Southern wealth and transformed Southern agriculture. For the Confederacy, the experience of war wore at the very foundations of their state's rationale, leading white Southerners to wonder whether it was worth risking their lives to create a nation-state that increasingly resembled the one they had left.

The 4th United States Colored Infantry stand for inspection. After the Emancipation Proclamation, a number of African American regiments were created. Despite initial concerns, they soon proved themselves as able fighters at Milliken's Bend and Battery Wagner.

The Confederate massacre of African American soldiers at Fort Pillow in April 1864 was a horrifying event but saw no reprisal from Lincoln.

FRANK LESLIE'S ILLUSTRATED

NEWSPAPER

Entered according to Act of Congress in the year 1864, by FRANK LESLIE, in the Clerk's Office of the District Court for the Southern District of New York.

No. 449—Vol. XVIII.]　　　　NEW YORK, MAY 7, 1864.　　　　[TERMS: $3.50 YEARLY, 14 WEEKS $1.00.

THE WAR IN LOUISIANA—VIEW OF NATCHITOCHES.—FROM A SKETCH BY OUR SPECIAL ARTIST, C. E. H. BONWILL.—SEE PAGE 102.

THE WAR IN TENNESSEE—REBEL MASSACRE OF THE UNION TROOPS AFTER THE SURRENDER AT FORT PILLOW, APRIL 12.—SEE PAGE 102.

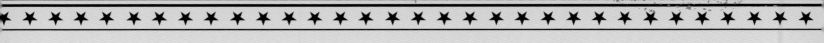

At the Battle of Cold Harbor in June 1864 the Union forces failed to overcome the Confederate defenses, despite a significant numerical advantage.

CHAPTER 7
1864:
YEAR OF DECISION

EVERYONE UNDERSTOOD just how important 1864 would be. Abraham Lincoln would stand for re-election in a contest that would serve as a referendum on the progress of the war in the eyes of Northern voters. Moreover, the president decided to stake his all on the shoulders of Ulysses S. Grant, whom he brought to Washington in March to take over as general-in-chief of the armies of the United States. It would be left to the victor of Vicksburg and Chattanooga to devise a strategy that would at a minimum convince everyone that the Union was destined to prevail in time for Northern voters to give Father Abraham four more years.

The Confederate high command was well aware of the situation. In Virginia, Robert E. Lee still entertained thoughts of resuming offensive operations, perhaps after first stymieing another Union general's operational plan. His target was Northern civilian morale and the electoral fortunes of the Lincoln administration. Yet there were other

places in the Confederacy to defend, and with dwindling manpower and resources, it seemed increasingly evident that a failure to prevail in 1864 might well result in the disintegration of the effort to achieve Southern independence. No more would there be discussion about foreign intervention: events in Europe, including the slow emergence of Germany under Bismarck, were now uppermost in the minds of English and French policymakers. However, a Democratic triumph in the 1864 presidential contest would indicate a loss of support for the Union war effort and point the way to a settlement short of Southern surrender.

Grant Takes Command

In December 1863, Illinois Congressman Elihu B. Washburne introduced a bill in Congress to revive the rank of lieutenant general,

Ulysses S. Grant at his headquarters in Cold Harbor, Virginia, June 1864.

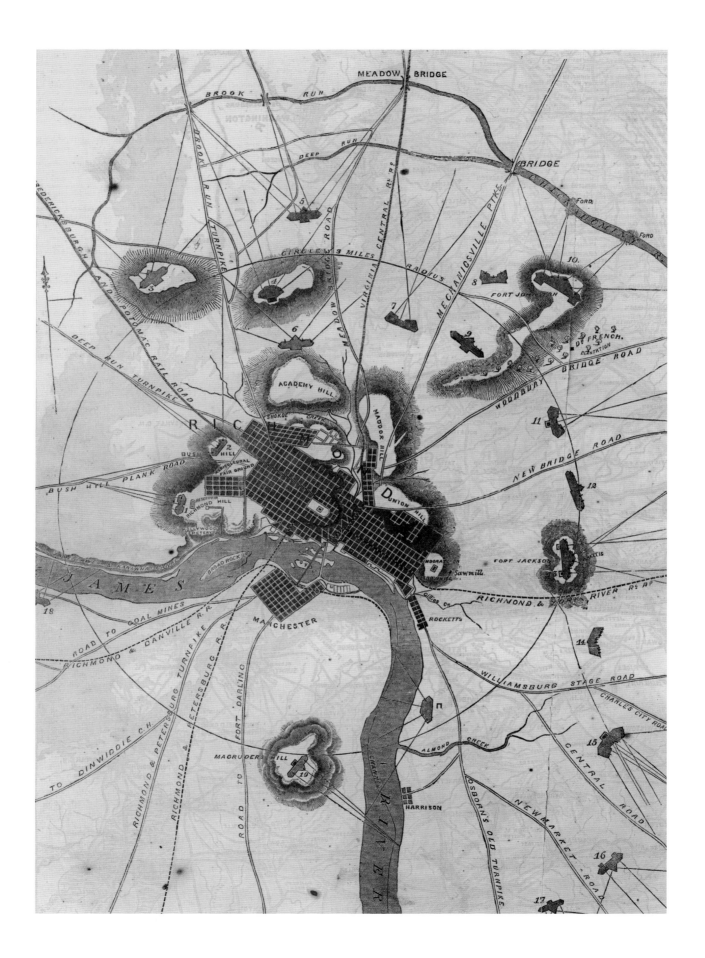

A map showing the defenses and railroads of Richmond, published in Harper's Weekly *in May 1864.*

once held by George Washington. He intended that it be awarded to his constituent, Ulysses S. Grant, who would thus outrank every officer in the United States Army. At first the Lincoln administration did not endorse the measure as it was debated in Congress, for the president was wary of elevating an individual who might prove to be a political rival on the eve of a presidential election. Only when Lincoln received assurances from Grant himself, transmitted through third parties, of the general's lack of political ambition did he support the measure with the intent of naming Grant as general-in-chief.

Initially Grant mapped out an innovative approach to crushing the Confederacy. He planned to keep continuous pressure on the Confederacy on multiple fronts. This would take the form of an amphibious attack against Mobile, Alabama, while William T. Sherman would drive south from Chattanooga to attack Confederate forces defending the critical rail junction of Atlanta, Georgia. His plans for the eastern theater were even more ambitious: leaving the majority of the Army of the Potomac to keep Lee's Army of Northern Virginia in check, he proposed to invade North Carolina, where he would liberate slaves, attract the support of disaffected Confederates and white unionists, and sever the railroads linking Richmond to the Confederate interior. Such plans proved too daring for Lincoln and Henry W. Halleck. They shelved the Mobile proposal, preferring a thrust westward into Louisiana to rally support for the state's Unionist government in which Lincoln had taken such a strong interest. They also objected to Grant's North Carolina operation, citing manpower concerns, but just as much because Lincoln preferred a direct confrontation with Lee in central Virginia between Washington and Richmond.

Thus admonished, Grant revised and modified his plan. He would await a more propitious moment to mount an operation against Mobile, leaving Sherman to shoulder the responsibility for challenging the Confederates in Georgia. Denied his North Carolina option, he formulated a four-pronged plan of attack in Virginia. One force

Major General Franz Sigel was one of many recent immigrants who fought on the Union side in the Civil War. Though he had previous military experience, it was his ability to recruit and command German-speaking soldiers that was most valued.

would sweep southward through the Shenandoah Valley, blocking it to the Confederacy as a source of supplies and as a way to threaten Washington. A second force would operate in southwest Virginia, capturing resources and severing railroad links. A third army would move up the James River toward Richmond to threaten the Confederate capital, while a fourth force, featuring the Army of the Potomac, would operate against Lee in central Virginia. The Confederate commander, deprived of the Shenandoah Valley, would have to choose between battling the Army of the Potomac and protecting Richmond. Grant hoped to force the foe into desperate and risky measures.

Yet even then Grant would have to recognize political reality in an election year. Back in 1861 Lincoln had appointed generals whose primary value was their perceived political clout, not military ability. By 1864 several of these generals had achieved seniority and would have to be assigned commands: to remove them altogether threatened to dissolve whatever sense of loyalty

they had for Lincoln. Thus the James River operation was entrusted to Benjamin F. Butler, a Massachusetts Democrat-turned-Republican who always sought out what was best for himself. Franz Sigel, a German immigrant with some military experience but an uneven record during the Civil War, secured the Shenandoah Valley assignment, while Nathaniel P. Banks, another Massachusetts politician, took charge of the Louisiana campaign. The fate of Grant's overall plan

depended in part on whether these three generals fulfilled their missions.

It soon became evident that Banks was bound to disappoint. He commenced his campaign prior to Grant assuming overall command, advancing into central Louisiana along the Red River. His men busied themselves with collecting cotton, while Banks did what he could to support the emergence of a Unionist state government. In April, the Confederates

Nathaniel P. Banks was more of a politician than a soldier. He had served as governor of Massachusetts until January 1861 but had no military experience—a fact that rankled many of the more accomplished veterans he had been promoted over.

The Battle of Pleasant Hill on April 9, 1864 was one of many costly engagements during the Red River Campaign.

The Battle of the Wilderness was the opening salvo in Grant's "Overland Campaign" but the result was a stalemate, resulting in high casualties for both sides.

counterattacked, driving Banks back, and before long the campaign was abandoned with little to show for it. Grant secured Banks's removal, but it was too late. Mobile would have to wait.

Overall, Grant's strategy, designed to achieve political as well as military success in timely fashion (the two were intertwined), found itself handicapped by the need to employ generals who owed their appointments to their supposed political importance. The failure of these generals in the field complicated Grant's task, since defeat damaged public confidence and support which would be expressed when voters went to the polls to select a president. Much would be made of the resources placed at Grant's disposal by Lincoln and the administration, but they could not give him what he needed most: time. The issue was not simply whether Grant would win eventually, but whether he could do so in time to give Abraham Lincoln a second term.

Grant vs Lee

On May 4, Grant commenced his campaign against Lee. George G. Meade's Army of the Potomac and Ambrose Burnside's IX Corps started crossing the Rapidan and Rappahannock rivers. Initially Grant hoped to make his way south of the Wilderness before turning west to engage Lee in the vicinity of the Mine Run battlefield of the previous December, but the Confederate commander refused to cooperate. The Army of Northern Virginia moved quickly eastward to engage Grant in the Wilderness, hoping to nullify the Union advantage in artillery and make the most of the tangled wooded terrain. When lead elements of the opposing armies made contact on the morning of May 5. Grant decided to accept the challenge. Over the next two days both sides struck telling blows, but in each case the defenders rallied, resulting in a bloody stalemate.

At first it seemed to be the same old story: the Confederates had checked a Union offensive thrust south of the Rapidan-Rappahannock river line. In the past the enemy had decided to withdraw, bringing the offensive to a sudden end. But Grant would not be deterred. On the evening of May 7, he began abandoning his position, but this time he directed his men southward, advancing once more toward Richmond. Lee hurried to block Grant once more at Spotsylvania Court House. For a dozen days Grant launched a series of assaults, several times coming close to dealing a devastating blow. However, Lee proved equal to the challenge, and once more Grant had to decide what to do next.

A photograph taken of the Wilderness battlefield in 1864.

At Spotsylvania Court House, the Army of Northern Virginia, led by Robert E. Lee, clashed with Grant's Army of the Potomac, which counted nearly twice as many soldiers. The decisive victory Grant had been hoping for continued to elude him.

With the contest between Grant and Lee entering its third week, it was clear that the nature of the war in Virginia was undergoing a fundamental transformation. As the fighting in the Wilderness subsided, Grant took aside a reporter who planned to return to Washington and asked him for a favor: "If you see the President, tell him from me that whatever happens, there will be no turning back." Grant was true to his word: a week into the campaign he assured his superiors, "I propose to fight it out on this line if it takes all summer." In the past, offensive operations had featured maneuvers to bring the foe to battle, with the ensuing combat taking place over at most several days. Grant proposed to keep up the pressure, probing for weak spots before fighting, then resuming operations immediately in a

relentless pattern of near-continuous combat. Lee parried each enemy thrust, barely avoiding disaster upon occasion, and rode to the front several times to rally his retreating men.

Events elsewhere forced Grant to make adjustments to his plan. His hopes that Union forces could finally take control of the Shenandoah Valley faded when the Confederates triumphed at New Market on May 15: before long, Lee was receiving reinforcements from the Valley. Although Benjamin F. Butler moved his Army of the James up its namesake river to land south of Richmond, he failed to press his early advantage, and Confederates under P. G. T. Beauregard soon blocked the way to Richmond, freeing Lee from concerns that the Confederate capital was in danger so that he could concentrate on

defeating Grant. Operations in southwest Virginia yielded little. The Union commander improvised, deciding to press southward once more to threaten Richmond himself. By the beginning of June, he had moved his men just a dozen miles east of Richmond, revisiting the ground where Lee had driven McClellan away from Richmond nearly two years earlier.

Convinced that he had damaged Lee's army so severely that one last blow might prove decisive, Grant planned to attack Lee's lines west of a small crossroads known as Cold Harbor. Delays in moving the attacking forces into position, however, gave Lee the opportunity to fortify, while Union commanders failed to make detailed preparations, such as reconnoitering the Confederate lines. The resulting assault on June 3 proved futile. Grant abandoned the attack when it became apparent that nothing would be achieved. He then turned to the option he had held in reserve while planning the spring campaign: he would swing southward once more, cross the James River, and advance upon Petersburg, a critical rail junction some 24 miles south of Richmond. Taking Petersburg would place Richmond in jeopardy and probably force its evacuation. However, once more Union forces fell just short of their objective, as

Beauregard, reinforced by Lee, staved off the weary attackers, who were beginning to feel the impact of some 40 days of combat. Thwarted once more, Grant decided to pin Lee against Richmond and Petersburg, digging entrenchments and establishing a supply depot, all the while looking for weaknesses to exploit and opportunities to keep the pressure on Lee.

"We must destroy this army of Grant's before he gets to the James River," Lee remarked to Jubal Early as June began. "If he gets there,

A pontoon bridge across the James River, 1864.

A Confederate gun at Battery Dantzler, part of the fortifications protecting the turnpike and railroad connecting Richmond and Petersburg. These earthworks, known as the Howlett line, played an important role in repulsing the Army of the James in May 1864.

it will become a siege, and then it will be a mere question of time." But Lee did not plan to go so quietly. He detached Early with a force sufficient to thwart another Union thrust through the Shenandoah; when the retreating Union forces opened up a way for Early to threaten Washington, Lee approved, and Confederate forces reached the outskirts of the Union capital on July 11, only to withdraw when reinforcements sent by Grant appeared just in time. Early's raid contributed to a growing sense among many Northerners that the bright promise of the spring was wilting in the summer heat, raising questions about whether the Lincoln administration could be trusted to bring the war to a victorious conclusion—not a welcome speculation in an election year. At the end of the month matters grew worse when a Union effort

to dig a mineshaft underneath Confederate lines near Petersburg, fill it with explosives, and blow a hole in the lines, opening a clear avenue for a Union advance, proved abortive. The Battle of the Crater, as it soon became known, was an embarrassing and bloody setback for Grant, featuring incompetent generalship and the misuse of African American troops.

As August began, Union victory seemed as far off as ever. Lee might be right that it would be a matter of time before Richmond fell, but time was one thing Grant did not have if he had to secure victories in advance of Lincoln's election. The most he could hope for was to keep Lee pinned in his trenches, depriving the Confederate commander of a chance to achieve a reversal of fortune through a characteristic counterattack.

Fort Sedgwick, outside Petersburg, Virginia. Its trenches bore a remarkable resemblance to those that would be seen in World War I.

Jubal Early was a thorn in the side of Union commanders for much of 1864. After the war ended, he continued to espouse the virtues of the Confederacy and helped establish the "Lost Cause" ideology.

The Road to Atlanta

While Grant and Lee wrestled in Virginia, in Georgia a somewhat different pattern emerged as William T. Sherman directed three field armies against the Army of Tennessee, with Joseph E. Johnston returning to field command. Sherman's supply depot at Chattanooga was less than 120 miles from Atlanta, but the nature of the terrain limited what he could do: while Grant could supply his army by water, Sherman had to rely upon railroads in the Confederate interior.

At the same time, Johnston was dependent on the same rail line stretching back from his army to Atlanta. Thus Sherman's plan was to use his superior numbers to outflank Johnston, threaten his supply line, and force him to fight or retreat; in turn, Johnston preferred withdrawing to attacking. Throughout May Sherman forced Johnston back, although Johnston did manage to make a stand at the end of the month that delayed the Union advance; a second series of advances and withdrawals came to a halt in late June, when Sherman launched an ill-fated assault

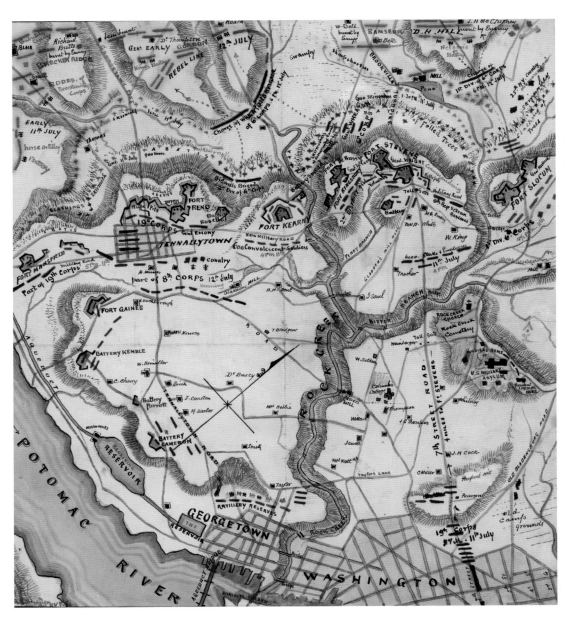

Jubal Early's plan of attack on Washington.

against Confederate fortified lines at Kennesaw Mountain on June 27. The Confederate success proved short-lived, and by the beginning of July Union forces were approaching the outskirts of Atlanta.

While the confrontation between Sherman and Johnston was far less costly in terms of casualties than was the contest between Grant and Lee, the result seemed familiar: Confederate forces were defending major rail centers against superior Union forces who sought to outflank the foe and stretch his defenses to breaking point using their superior numbers. The difference was that while Jefferson Davis trusted that Robert E. Lee would seek to reverse his army's fortunes (witness Early threatening Washington), he had no such faith in Johnston. After all, in 1862 Johnston had withdrawn before McClellan's advance until the armies were close to Richmond before finally attacking; the same pattern seemed to be repeating itself.

John Bell Hood was an aggressive, perhaps even reckless, Confederate general.

In 1862 fate had intervened, with an aggressive Lee replacing a seriously wounded Johnston; this time Davis would not wait for fate. He proposed to replace Johnston with corps commander John Bell Hood, who had earned a reputation as an aggressive brigade and division commander under Lee before he was twice seriously wounded, at Gettysburg and Chickamauga. Before making the move, Davis consulted with Lee, who praised Hood's aggressiveness but was unsure whether Hood possessed the other qualities needed in an army commander. Davis decided that a change had to be made.

No sooner had Hood assumed command than he set about driving the invaders away from Atlanta. In a series of attacks, however, the best he could do was to slow Sherman down, and at serious cost. Nevertheless, by the end of July it looked as if the stalemate around Atlanta mirrored that outside Richmond and Petersburg, with Grant and Sherman aiming to sever Confederate rail links. If the Confederates could hold on, discouraging Northern voters about the prospects for ultimate victory, Lincoln might face defeat at the polls.

Lincoln's Struggles

Lincoln rather easily secured renomination, deftly undermining the efforts of rivals such as Secretary of the Treasury Salmon P. Chase to present themselves as alternatives. Nor did he object to the naming of Tennessee's Andrew Johnson as his running mate when Republicans met in Baltimore in June, although it remains an open question as to how active he was in the selection process. But a military situation characterized by stalemates and setbacks augured ill for the fall contest. Moreover, the administration suffered embarrassment when it allowed newspaper editor Horace Greeley to meet with Confederate representatives supposedly empowered to negotiate a peace settlement on the basis of reunion and emancipation. In truth, these Confederate representatives were engaged in assisting the Democratic opposition to Lincoln, and jumped on the opportunity presented by Greeley's ill-fated mission to claim that Lincoln insisted upon emancipation as a precondition for peace, giving weight to the suggestion that white lives would continue to be sacrificed to secure blacks' freedom.

Facing charges that the war effort was a failure, several Republican leaders argued that it was time to abandon emancipation as a precondition for a negotiated settlement. They claimed that under no conditions could Northern voters be told that it was a black man's war but a white man's fight. Well aware that Jefferson Davis and the Confederate leadership would not abandon their quest for independence, a precondition for an acceptable negotiated peace, Lincoln weighed and then rejected any proposal that would set emancipation aside. He knew that unless slavery

was abolished, any peace settlement achieving reunion would be at best temporary, for the issue of slavery would continue to wear away at the bonds of union.

Much though Lincoln abhorred the institution of slavery, his reasoning reflected his awareness of the importance of African American military service to the Union war effort. At a time when fewer white men volunteered for service and whites conscripted into service either deserted or often proved poor fighting men, the presence of black men in blue uniforms—nearly one in seven Union soldiers were black—was critical. These men had given their lives on the battlefield, and at Fort Pillow they had been slaughtered while attempting to surrender. They did so because of Lincoln's promise that they would be free. "Why should they give their lives for us, with full notice of our purpose to betray them?" asked Lincoln. "Drive back to the support of the rebellion the physical force which the colored people now give, and promise us, and neither the present, nor any coming administration, can save the Union." The president's word was his bond. Should he return black soldiers to slavery, he told two White House visitors, "I should be damned in time and in

The Battle of Kennesaw Mountain was a significant defeat for the Union forces, but ultimately it failed to prevent the advance of Sherman's forces towards Atlanta.

Above: Soldiers of the 107th United States Colored Troops. African Americans formed a crucial component of the Union war effort, and Lincoln was well aware of their contributions.

Below: Édouard Manet's painting of the battle between the Kearsarge *and the* Alabama *near Cherbourg, France. Confederate raiders often sought shelter in the neutral ports of the United Kingdom and France.*

eternity for so doing. The world shall know that I will keep my faith to friends & enemies, come what will."

Yet Lincoln also believed that the prospect for his re-election remained dim. Union naval victories did little to change that. In June the USS *Kearsarge* had tracked down the legendary Confederate commerce raider the CSS *Alabama* off the coast of Cherbourg, France, and sunk it; at the beginning of August Admiral David G. Farragut had led his squadron into Mobile Bay. When an ironclad struck a mine (then called a torpedo) and sank, Farragut rallied his sailors, crying, "Damn the torpedoes! Full speed ahead!" However dramatic these triumphs might be, they did little to counterbalance the feeling that a strategic stalemate persisted. That impression fostered a sentiment that Lincoln was doomed, and he agreed. Meeting with his cabinet on August 23, he asked them to sign a folded sheet of paper, preventing them from seeing what was written inside: "This morning, as for some days past, it seems exceedingly probable that this Administration will not be re-elected. Then it will be my duty to so cooperate with the President elect, as to save the Union between the election and inauguration; as he will have secured his election on such ground that he cannot possibly save it afterwards."

Dire words, these; but they seemed appropriate under the circumstances. A week later, as the Democrats gathered in Chicago to nominate a presidential candidate, their platform declared: "After four years of failure to restore the Union by the experiment of war, we demand that immediate efforts be made for a cessation of hostilities, with a view to an ultimate convention of the states, or other peaceable means, to the end that, at the earliest practicable moment, peace may be restored on the basis of the Federal Union." With that on the table, they nominated George B. McClellan to head the ticket. Although the party's standard bearer would not hear of abandoning the war effort short of victory, his performance on the battlefield led one to doubt that he could realize that vision. As August drew to a close, the continued existence

Union soldiers by captured guns in the fort at Atlanta, 1864.

of the Union and the promise of emancipation both seemed in peril.

Sherman and Sheridan

In the early morning of September 3, 1864, a telegraph in Georgia began sending a message. It was time for William T. Sherman to update his progress. For over a month his armies had moved around Atlanta, destroying railroads and cutting the city and its Confederate defenders off from the rest of the Confederacy. Realizing that he was about to be surrounded and isolated, John Bell Hood decided it was time to abandon the city. He did so on the night of September 1, and Union forces entered the city the next day. "So Atlanta is ours, and fairly won," Sherman declared.

In that moment stalemate gave way to success. Grant's strategy had paid off: the Confederacy had given way somewhere. That Sherman had already effectively eliminated Atlanta in terms of its military value by destroying the rail links out of the city—and that Hood had escaped—meant little to a Northern public that saw the occupation of key cities as signposts of victory. Democrats crying that the war was a failure choked on their words. To be sure, Hood remained a threat to Sherman: for weeks to come he would shift northward in an effort to break Sherman's railroad supply line back to Chattanooga. Such activity made Sherman wonder whether possession of Atlanta was now an albatross around his neck, and he began to contemplate his next move.

Before long, there was more news, this time from Virginia. Back in August, Grant had decided that it was time to deal with the Shenandoah Valley and Jubal Early's army. He assigned cavalryman Philip H. Sheridan to take charge of the assorted forces in northern Virginia and Maryland, forge them into a single force, and march southward once more through the area with orders to defeat Early and lay waste to the valley. However, Sheridan took his time organizing his command. Growing impatient, Grant travelled to Sheridan's headquarters in the aftermath of Sherman's victory, only to discover upon his arrival that Sheridan was now ready to begin his campaign. On September 19 he smashed Early's army at Winchester, Virginia; three days later he followed up by delivering another damaging blow at Fisher's Hill. Early retreated southward to refit and reorganize, while Sheridan commenced his destruction of Confederate resources. Once more Northern newspapers celebrated a major victory; once more the Democratic platform was discredited by events. Military victory brightened Lincoln's political prospects.

In the past Confederates had looked to Robert E. Lee to restore the situation. That he was unable to do so was testimony to Grant's success in taking Lee out of the war by pinning him against Richmond and Petersburg. Through early October the Confederate high command struggled to no avail to turn the tide once more, in order to avoid defeat at the polls, but in mid-October state elections in Ohio, Indiana, and Pennsylvania presaged a Lincoln triumph in November. Early decided on one last effort to salvage the situation.

Philip Sheridan's victories against Jubal Early in September 1864 provided a much needed morale boost for the Union.

"Sheridan's Ride" at the Battle of Cedar Creek on October 19, 1864 was widely celebrated in art and popular culture.

An 1864 presidential election campaign banner depicting Abraham Lincoln and his running mate, Andrew Johnson. Yet despite the overwhelming victory in the electoral college, the closer race in the popular vote indicates that the result was far from inevitable.

and any advantage Early might have gained would have been temporary. Instead, Sheridan's triumph clinched the case for enthusiastic optimism among those Northern voters who still harbored doubts about the eventual success of the cause.

On Election Day 1864, Abraham Lincoln overwhelmed McClellan in the Electoral College by a vote of 212 to 21. The president secured 55 percent of the popular vote. Yet a careful examination of the results revealed the durability of Democratic support for McClellan, even in the wake of a string of Union victories; the Electoral College margin magnified the extent of Lincoln's success. Still, with Lincoln re-elected, Confederates faced the fact that the war would continue with renewed determination. The likelihood of Confederacy survival had dwindled, and it was hard to see how to prevent its complete collapse.

He planned to attack Sheridan's unsuspecting army south of Winchester along Cedar Creek. That Sheridan himself was away from his command on a visit to Washington seemed to offer Early an opportunity he could not pass up.

In the pre-dawn hours of October 19, the Confederates advanced, driving the enemy back. Early believed he was on the verge of a decisive victory. Even as Union forces rallied, they were surprised to see Sheridan galloping in their midst, waving his hat and shouting encouragement. He had arrived at Winchester the previous evening, and in the morning set out to make the 20-mile trip to rejoin his men, quickening his pace when he learned of Early's attack. What became known as "Sheridan's Ride" was celebrated in song, story, and painting; his dramatic return was a prelude to an afternoon attack that drove Early away in complete defeat. The inspirational victory meant little in strictly military terms, for Sheridan had largely accomplished his mission,

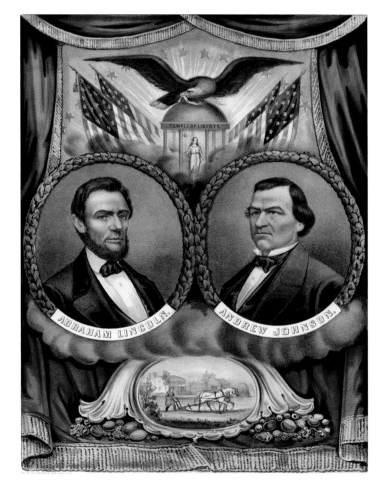

The Confederate Government, led by Jefferson Davis, flees Richmond on April 2, 1865. The Confederate defenders were ordered to burn the strategic resources of the city, including warehouses, armories, and bridges, but the blaze soon spread throughout the city.

CHAPTER 8
TOWARD VICTORY AND PEACE

The re-election of Abraham Lincoln destroyed Confederate hopes for a negotiated compromise peace with an incoming Democratic administration. Union military operations no longer had to consider the election calendar: Grant now had the time to map out a strategy that would close out the Confederacy systematically. Lincoln could now renew his push for emancipation, embodied now in the ratification of a constitutional amendment that abolished the "peculiar institution" once and for all everywhere in the United States. Still, in a war of reunion, how the conflict ended could shape the peace to follow, and the more consent the victors could obtain from the vanquished, the easier it would be to achieve the sort of peace that would lead to real reunion.

Yet not all Confederates had lost hope. To date the experiment in Southern nationhood had been founded upon the premise that independence was the best way to preserve and protect slavery, and the Confederacy served primarily as a means to that end. Now, however, after years of bitter and bloody warfare, for some people the Confederacy had become an end in itself, although how that independence would be achieved and what a postwar Confederacy would look like remained as elusive as ever. But would Confederate victory require the destruction of the very reason it was created in the first place? In the aftermath of Lincoln's victory, would slavery have to give way so that the Confederacy would survive.

Sherman to the Sea

Within weeks of capturing Atlanta William T. Sherman realized that the city was little more than an albatross around his neck.

The March to the Sea terrorized the population of the South as Sherman aimed to show the Confederates that "war and individual ruin are synonymous."

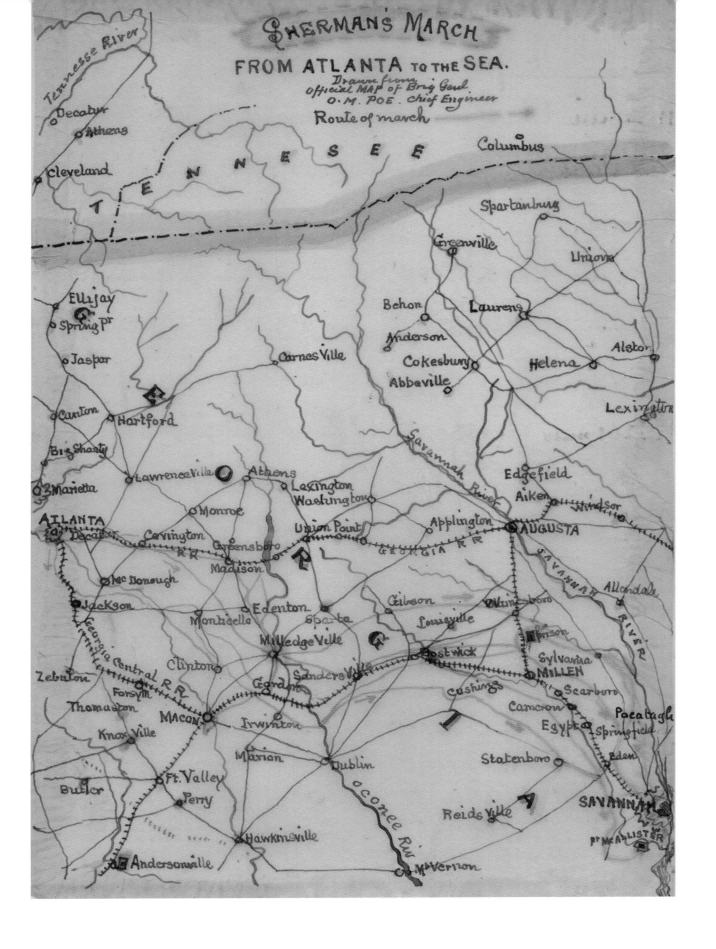

*A map showing the route
of Sherman's March to the
Sea, which lasted from
November 15 to December
21, 1864.*

To keep his army supplied he had to depend on keeping open the railroad back to Chattanooga, which meant spreading out his men to guard it against Hood's Army of Tennessee. Yet once Atlanta's status as a rail hub was eliminated, what reason remained to hold it? As withdrawal was out of the question, Sherman reasoned, why not advance through Georgia? He could replicate Grant's Vicksburg campaign by living off the land and using wagons to carry essential supplies; he could march through the Confederate heartland, demonstrating to its citizens that their government could no longer protect them. "I propose to demonstrate the vulnerability of the South, and make its inhabitants feel that war and individual ruin are synonymous terms," he explained, later adding, "This may not be war, but rather statesmanship." A march might wreak havoc upon

*Sherman's troops destroy
the railroad in Atlanta
before they leave.*

Confederate resources and infrastructure, but it would also sear Confederate morale.

Ulysses S. Grant was not so sure. Better, he thought, to take care of Hood's army first, lest it be left to its own devices, including undertaking a march of its own. Over time, however, he came to appreciate just how difficult it would be for Sherman to chase Hood down. So long as Sherman left behind sufficient force to keep Hood from making too much mischief, he could proceed with his plan. Still, there was no need for Sherman to commence such an operation prior to the presidential election, lest a setback undo the impact capturing Atlanta had made on northern voters' minds. Sherman was also open to other approaches, at one point suggesting to Georgia's governor Joseph Brown that if Brown, who had often feuded with Davis's Richmond regime, withdrew Georgia from the Confederacy altogether, he would tell his men to restrain themselves and would compensate civilians for any property he confiscated. When that idea fell apart, he returned to his notions of rough treatment, even as he knew that an army living off the land needed to seek new sources of food every day, necessitating a campaign of continuous movement.

Sherman waited until mid-November, well after election day, to embark on his march. Leaving Atlanta in flames, he ventured southward, at first keeping his ultimate destination a secret, although it was understood that he would target a port where he could secure supplies. In the end he headed for Savannah. His men targeted plantations, food supplies, railroads, and other enemy targets, living off the land; some soldiers who straggled and wandered, known as bummers, were even less disciplined in their behavior, although on the whole the Union soldiers behaved when it came to refraining from physically harming white civilians,

especially women (African American women were more likely to be assaulted and attacked). However, not all the chaos was due to the behavior of Sherman's men: Confederate cavalry under the command of Joseph Wheeler spread their own brand of chaos and destruction around Confederate civilians. If the march angered and terrified civilians, it may have done more damage to the morale of Georgia's Confederates at the front, who had enlisted to protect home and family only to see them come under attack: Lee declined to issue them furloughs home for fear that they would never come back.

After a month of marching, Sherman's columns reached the outskirts of Savannah, Georgia. Its defenders managed to escape capture but left the city defenseless; the officials surrendered the city without resistance, and Sherman refrained from inflicting damage on it. He delighted in proffering the city as a Christmas gift to President Lincoln. However, what made the celebration even more joyous was the news that John Bell Hood's Army of Tennessee had met with a disastrous fate. For as Sherman had headed southward, Hood had moved northward from Alabama, heading for Nashville, Tennessee, and points north, maybe as far as the Ohio River. Frustrated by the failure of his subordinates to trap errant Union forces at Spring Hill, Tennessee, Hood rashly ordered them to attack Franklin, where Union defenders

beat back assault after assault while inflicting significant casualties upon the foe. Once more Hood's aggressiveness proved counterproductive and costly. The Confederates dragged themselves northward to Nashville, where George H. Thomas was busily assembling a patchwork army with which to end Hood's adventure. Confounded by severe weather, Thomas decided to make sure he was fully prepared to move, aggravating Grant, who wanted action and assumed that Hood could make more mischief (which, had he not already wrecked his army, might well have been the case). Grant was on the brink of replacing Thomas personally when he learned that Thomas had at last delivered a hard blow that in two days smashed Hood's ragged army and drove what remained of it southward. Although, contrary to legend, Thomas had not destroyed Hood's army—a stalled pursuit prevented that outcome—he had eliminated whatever offensive threat it posed. All in all, it was a season of success.

Joseph Wheeler, a Confederate cavalry commander, inflicted suffering on the population of Georgia too.

The coat of Confederate general Patrick Cleburne, worn at the time of his death in the Battle of Franklin.

Seeking Peace and Destroying Slavery

As the war entered its fourth year, slavery as an institution was struggling to survive. The combined impact of the friction of war, the progress of Union arms, congressional measures, Lincoln's Emancipation Proclamation, and the earnest efforts of the enslaved to seek freedom had eroded what was once deemed the cornerstone of the Confederacy. Meanwhile, Maryland and Missouri ended slavery through state action; Andrew Johnson made sure to declare the institution destroyed before he left Tennessee to take the oath of office as vice president. But slavery remained a legal institution in Delaware and Kentucky, and many enslaved people endured in parts of the South still under Confederate control, some having been moved away from the Yankees by their owners. Should the war end suddenly, the status of the Emancipation Proclamation as a war measure would be in question, although Lincoln had made sure that the Supreme Court would not overturn the measure when he nominated his

former treasury secretary, the staunchly antislavery Salmon P. Chase, to replace the deceased Roger B. Taney as Chief Justice of the Supreme Court. Lincoln now turned to what he termed a "king's cure" to eliminate slavery throughout the United States through constitutional amendment. With re-election secured, he could swing whatever deals he had to make to ensure that the amendment would make its way through the House of Representatives, claiming victory as January 1865 came to an end.

At the same time, Confederate proposals for enlisting slaves as soldiers enjoyed new popularity. At the beginning of the war, free blacks and creoles in several Southern locales, notably New Orleans and Alabama, worried that they might be subject to scrutiny and repression by white Southerners concerned about insurrection, had volunteered to support the Confederate cause, but Confederate authorities summarily dismissed such initiatives. However, Confederate armies had used enslaved blacks to support military operations as cooks, wagon drivers, officers' servants, and in other

The Battle of Franklin was a military disaster for John Bell Hood and the Army of Tennessee.

capacities, although never as soldiers. Some Confederates favored exploring the possibility of using black slaves as combat soldiers: at the beginning of 1864 Confederate general Patrick Cleburne had pressed the issue, only to be silenced by Jefferson Davis. Now, with disasters staring them in the face, Confederates revisited the issue. Advocates of the idea pointed out that without such help, the Confederacy was probably doomed, while opponents argued that to arm slaves—a concept that struck fear into the hearts of many white Southerners—meant that the Confederacy no longer made any sense, given that it was formed to protect the very institution it now proposed to erode. Moreover, enlistment without emancipation made no sense, for it would deprive blacks of a reason to fight. While the Confederacy ultimately accepted the idea, it was too little, too late: a few dozen black recruits in Richmond never amounted to anything as a combat force.

Jefferson Davis was willing to go even further, however. Whatever the roots of his commitment to Southern independence, he was now willing to sacrifice slavery to help the Confederacy survive. In December 1864 he authorized Louisiana planter Duncan Kenner to travel to Europe, where he offered emancipation as the price the Confederacy was willing to pay for recognition (and hopefully intervention) by Great Britain and France. However, as European diplomacy toward the Confederacy had always rested upon an assessment of the Confederacy's chances of persisting, the mission was little more than a curious footnote. It looked as though the end was near.

There was talk of a negotiated peace as 1865 began. Francis P. Blair, Sr., a veteran of Washington politics who knew Davis from before the war, presented Lincoln with a proposal whereby the two sides would declare an armistice that would enable them to join forces to oust the French-supported regime of Maximilian of Mexico, who had been installed as emperor in 1864. That far-fetched idea would supposedly open the way for old foes to become friends again, leaving everything else to be settled peacefully. Lincoln was perfectly willing to see if Davis would accept his terms of the submission of Confederate armies, the destruction of slavery, and the reunification of the republic; Davis had no interest in acceding to those requirements. However, he was willing to dispatch a three-person commission headed by Confederate vice president Alexander H. Stephens to see if something could be done, in part because Davis was confident that Lincoln's insistence on his terms would remind Confederates of what was at stake. No sooner had Lincoln celebrated the passage through Congress of the Thirteenth Amendment than he agreed (at Grant's urging) to meet with Stephens and his fellow commissioners at Hampton Roads, off the coast of Fort Monroe, Virginia, where the *Monitor* and *Virginia* had clashed nearly two years before. Nothing came of the discussion, despite Lincoln's willingness to provide compensation for the loss of slavery and a phased-in emancipation. The war would go on.

A Confederate sergeant sits with his family slave. Slaves had provided an important source of labor for the South's war effort, but it was not until the final months of the war that the Confederacy risked allowing slaves to fight as soldiers.

The Vise Tightens

Grant had spent the weeks after Lincoln's reelection tightening his grip on Lee at Richmond and Petersburg. There was no need yet to mount another offensive; besides, Confederate strength was eroding through desertion, so much so that Grant seized upon the willingness of Confederate authorities to included captured black Union soldiers in prisoner exchanges in order to resume such exchanges after a year in which prisoners of war on both sides had suffered greatly in enemy prisons. Pinning Lee in place allowed Sherman, Thomas, and other Union generals the freedom to carry on against crumbling Confederate resistance. In January, an amphibious Union force took Fort Fisher, North Carolina, effectively shutting off the lone remaining Confederate port at Wilmington. Before long Grant reinforced that toehold along the North Carolina coast and advanced into the interior. He would wait until spring came and the roads dried to take care of Lee.

Francis Preston Blair, Sr., led a delegation to negotiate peace with President Lincoln, but his unwillingness to compromise on slavery brought the talks to a halt.

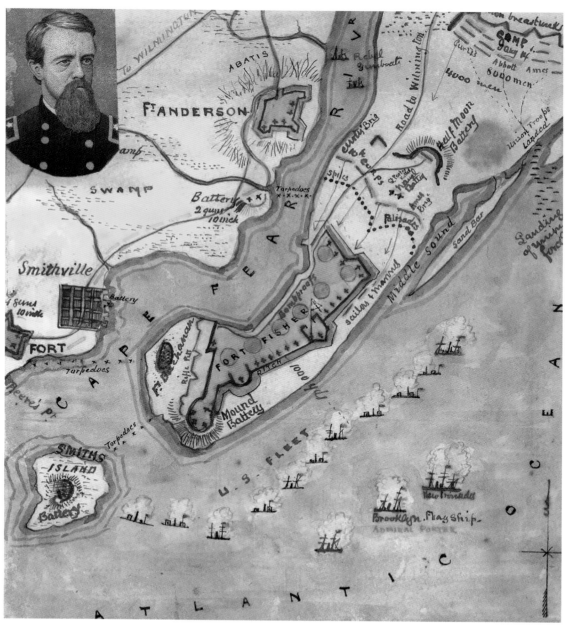

A map of the Union plan of attack on Fort Fisher, January 15, 1865.

The ruins of Columbia, South Carolina, shortly after the arrival of Sherman's army. The city burned as it changed hands, and Sherman was widely accused of ordering the conflagration at the time.

William T. Sherman planned to join up with those forces in North Carolina, but to do so he would first have to march through South Carolina, the cradle of secession. He recalled how white Georgians had implored Union forces to remember who really started the war and thus deserved the harshest treatment of all, and Sherman was disposed to oblige them. This time, however, he did not want his movements complicated by a flood of refugee blacks seeking protection from Union arms to make good their freedom. In mid-January he issued Special Field Order No. 15, confiscating some 400,000 acres of land along the Atlantic seacoast and making it available in plots of 40 acres for freed families to cultivate. Whether this was a temporary measure designed to free up Sherman's army to operate unencumbered or was a step in the direction of permanently providing land for the freedpeople remained to be seen; Sherman was no abolitionist, and his embrace of white supremacy was nearly as intense as his hatred of the Confederacy.

In early February Sherman commenced his march north through South Carolina. He confused Confederates as to his objective before leaving Charleston to its fate while turning toward the state capitol at Columbia, which burst into flames as the Confederate defenders left it and the Federals entered it. Much finger-pointing followed as Confederate commander Wade Hampton and Sherman each blamed their counterpart for the conflagration, which owed at least as much to the confusion of evacuation and the chaos of occupation. Charleston capitulated at the same time, and Sherman moved on to North Carolina, hooking up with Union forces already there after

advising his men to temper their aggressive and destructive behavior, which had enjoyed free rein in the Palmetto State. There Joseph Johnston, recently restored to field command, awaited him with what was left of the Army of Tennessee and other scattered forces. Although at one point Johnston attempted to check Sherman's advance, his failure at Bentonville demonstrated that the Confederates were in a difficult position as winter came to a close.

The Road to Appomattox ... and Beyond

Ulysses S. Grant decided not to undertake any major offensives against Robert E. Lee in the winter of 1864–5. It was enough to see Confederate strength eroding through desertion; by keeping Lee penned up in Richmond and Petersburg, Grant prevented him from disrupting the progress of Union arms elsewhere. The Confederate leader, who had been elevated to command of all the Confederate armies in February 1865, contemplated meeting with Grant with an eye toward crafting a negotiated peace in the form of a military convention, but Lincoln directed Grant not to consider the offer.

With the advent of spring and drier roads, Grant knew that Lee would have to do something. Lee shared that understanding. He proposed that if he could elude Grant by evacuating Richmond and Petersburg, joining forces with Johnston, and then attack Sherman, he might yet prolong the struggle, although to what end was not clear. However, his effort to force Grant to tighten his lines to set the stage for a rapid move failed when Union forces rather easily checked his offensive against Fort Stedman on March 25. Lee had hoped that a breakthrough, however short-lived, near Grant's headquarters at City Point, east of Petersburg where the Appomattox River emptied into the James River, would force Grant to retract his left flank, but such was not to be. Instead, the attack served to alert Grant to the notion that Lee was ready to move. The Union commander decided to sweep around the Confederate right once more and sever the last remaining railroad linking Richmond and Petersburg to points south. That operation, climaxing in Phil Sheridan's dramatic

victory at Five Forks on April 1, signaled the end to Confederate possession of Richmond. Petersburg fell on April 2; that night Lee evacuated Richmond, with the retreating Confederates setting fire to the city to prevent the Yankees from seizing anything important. The next day white Richmonders were greeted by the sight of black Union soldiers liberating the city's enslaved people, followed on April 4 by a visit from Abraham Lincoln, who had been visiting Grant's headquarters.

Grant had no interest in making a triumphant entrance into Richmond. He hurried his army west to cut off Lee's army before it had a chance to unite with Johnston or, failing that, to make it to the Blue Ridge Mountains. Over the next week the Armies of the Potomac and the James marched as hard as they ever had, while Lee's army began to collapse under the pressure of the pursuit, with hungry men dropping their weapons or just walking away. Lee's army nearly dissolved altogether when Grant smashed into his rear at Sayler's Creek on April 6; the following evening Grant called upon Lee to surrender. At first Lee hesitated, perhaps seeking to extract favorable terms, but more likely seeking to avoid giving in. However, when his army approached Appomattox Court House on the morning of April 9 he discovered that Grant had beaten him there and was on the point of surrounding him completely. It was time to go see Grant, although Lee admitted that he would rather "die a thousand deaths."

Accompanied by a single staff officer, Lee sat down in Wilmer McLean's parlor and awaited his fate. That was not by McLean's choice. Years earlier he had lived just south of Bull Run, but in the wake of two battles declared that he wanted to move where the war would not find him. Now it had. A short time later, Grant, accompanied by several generals and members of his staff, rode up to the house, dismounted, and walked into the house and the parlor just left of the front door. In abandoning his headquarters baggage several days earlier, Lee had decided to keep a sharp dress uniform and a presentation sword; in contrast, Grant, clad in a private's blouse with only his shoulder straps denoting his rank, had no sword,

Sheridan's dramatic victory at the Battle of Five Forks led to Union control of the Confederate capital of Richmond.

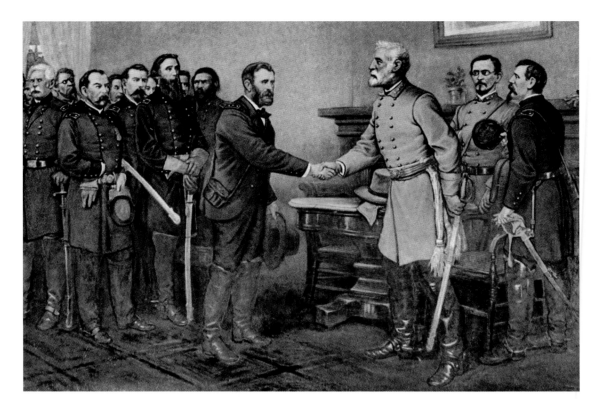

Robert E. Lee surrenders to Ulysses S. Grant at Appomattox Court House on April 9, 1865, effectively ending the Civil War.

while his boots were muddy from the morning ride as he hurried to meet Lee.

The conversation was short and somewhat strained. With no notes before him, Grant, who had recalled Lincoln's preference for a generous treatment of the defeated, provided that after the Confederates stacked arms, they would be allowed to go home, undisturbed by United States authorities so long as they remained law-abiding. Officers could keep their sidearms, meaning Lee would not have to give his sword to Grant (who would have had no use for it, anyway); later Grant provided for the distribution of rations to feed the hungry Confederates (rations Sheridan had captured in the previous 24 hours) and allowed them to take their animals home to assist in the spring plowing. This was far from the unconditional surrender Lee feared Grant would demand, and he readily accepted the terms. As for Grant, he realized that these terms were a first step toward peace, a peace he hoped white Southerners would accept without much bitterness or anger. As Lee left, Grant even lifted his hat in salute; later he told his men no to celebrate too loudly,

lest that humiliate the vanquished foe. After all, the Confederates were now their countrymen again, right?

By the time Confederate soldiers stacked their arms three days later, Grant and Lee had both left the scene, with Grant returning to Washington, where an elated Lincoln awaited him. Several days later Lincoln invited his general to accompany him to Ford's Theater, but Grant demurred, claiming that his wife and he needed to hurry to New Jersey to see their children… although in truth both the Grants feared that Mary Lincoln might make a scene at the attention given Grant instead of her husband, a concern rooted in several outbursts over the past several weeks.

The events of that evening, with Lincoln assassinated as he sat at the theater, cast a pall over the celebration of Lee's surrender, but it failed to interfere with ongoing military operations. Union forces had finally captured Mobile on April 12, the same day another column entered the Confederacy's first capital, Montgomery. Two days after Lincoln's death Sherman and Joe Johnston commenced negotiations outside of Durham, North Carolina, at

James Bennett's farm. Aware of Lincoln's preferences for a lenient peace and concerned that order be restored throughout the South as soon as possible, Sherman went far beyond his authority in framing an initial set of terms that exceeded military matters to talk of restoring state governments and leaving unclear the status of slavery. Once the authorities at Washington rejected these terms, Sherman, with Grant coming down to North Carolina to look over his shoulder, offered Johnston the same terms Grant had offered Lee, and Johnston accepted on April 26. Other surrenders soon followed. By the summer the Confederacy was no more, although most people understood that Appomattox was the death blow.

No one quite knew what was to come next. Blacks in the Confederacy believed peace meant freedom, and by year's end slavery would be as dead as the Confederacy. But what freedom meant and exactly how the Rebels would return to their former allegiance remained to be decided, and the answers would not come easily.

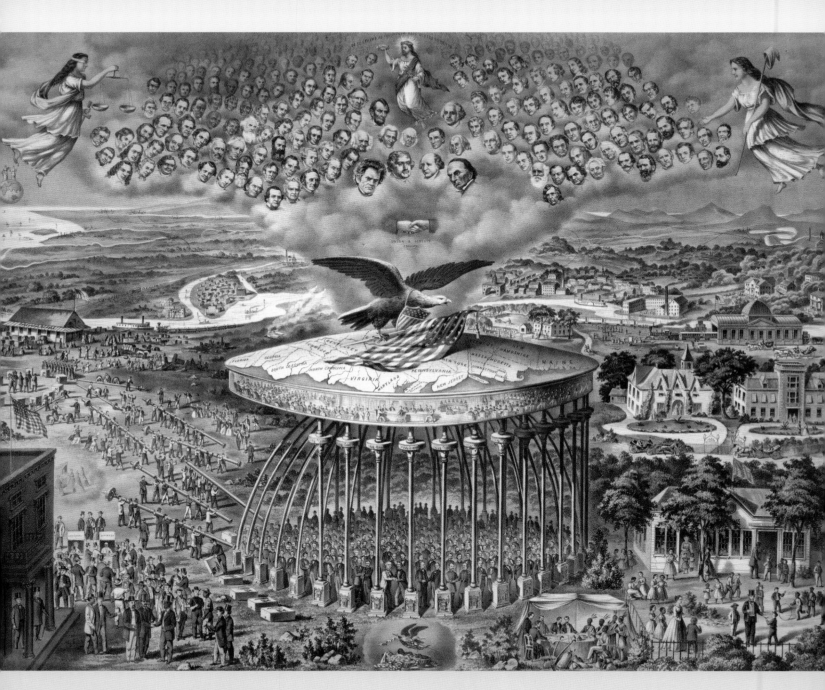

An allegory of the reconciliation of North and South through Reconstruction.

CHAPTER 9
RECONSTRUCTION UNDER LINCOLN AND JOHNSON

IN A SENSE, Reconstruction began during the secession winter of 1860–1. Compromise measures designed to counter secession included proposals that would have altered the republic's institutional structure to appease secessionists. Those efforts proved futile. In years to come, one of the major debates over Reconstruction would concern the meaning of the term itself. Was Reconstruction's aim to restore the republic, or would it be founded anew in ways that reflected the impact of war and eventually emancipation?

Moreover, as Reconstruction's scope expanded to include emancipation, it proved challenging to both formulate and implement a policy that sought to achieve both sectional reconciliation between whites (North and South), as well as equality, opportunity, and justice for black Americans (free as well as formerly enslaved). Most white Southerners defined reconciliation as requiring that they be left alone to handle black freedom as they desired in the most limited of ways, while efforts to promote the status of newly freed black people offended most white Southerners and not a few white Northerners.

Yet what happened during Reconstruction did much to define what the American Civil War did—and did not—achieve, and it established a legacy that Americans still wrestle with today.

Wartime Reconstruction Under Lincoln

During the conflict's early years, Abraham Lincoln, seeking ways to woo back Confederates by promising minimal changes, endeavored to construct loyalist regimes in those Confederate states where the Union had established a meaningful military presence. He enjoyed some success in Tennessee and Louisiana, made progress in Virginia, and struggled in Arkansas and North Carolina. By the summer of 1862, however, Lincoln was reconsidering his earlier belief that Southern Unionists could form governments that could attract alienated Confederates. Southern Unionists seemed more interested in protecting slavery than in taking the lead to form loyalist regimes: as emancipation gained traction as a Union war aim, many Southern Unionists assumed a low profile or warned Lincoln that emancipation would doom efforts to garner support among most Southern whites.

At the same time, the war to save the Union began to transform it, as the friction of military operations undermined slavery. Union military authorities struggled with how to handle the flood of black refugees that flooded their camps, seeking food, shelter, and protection. Such acts of self-emancipation doomed efforts to seek a revival of Southern Unionist sentiment which required that slavery be left untouched. For the moment, Union

elections, Lincoln would support seating the state's Congressional delegation in Congress.

Not all Republicans embraced this plan. Some sought greater guarantees for black rights while others wanted to punish former Confederates. Some objected that 10 percent was far too slim a foundation upon which to erect a viable state government. One bill, framed by Senator Benjamin F. Wade of Ohio and Congressman Henry Winter Davis of Maryland, would have required 50 percent of a state's 1860 electorate to return to the fold, despite the fact that only individuals who had never supported the Confederacy could vote or serve as delegates and officeholders in the reconstructed governments. These new regimes would have to abolish slavery, although Wade dropped a provision that would have enfranchised blacks. Lincoln rejected the measure as Congress's session came to a close in July 1864; his "pocket veto" meant that Congress could not override it as it was not in session.

What was on one hand an institutional struggle between president and Congress about which branch of the federal government was in charge of Reconstruction also represented a division within Republican ranks as to what that process would look like, especially when it came to questions of slavery and freedom as well as how to treat former Confederates. Some Republicans, led by Senator Charles Sumner of Massachusetts and Congressman Thaddeus Stevens of Pennsylvania, opposed what they believed was a hasty restoration of civil government in

During the war, Abraham Lincoln was eager to obtain the consent of the populations of Confederate territory occupied by Union forces, but soon found that some measure of reconstruction was needed.

Senator Benjamin Wade sponsored a bill which provided strict conditions for the re-entry of Confederate states to the political life of the Union.

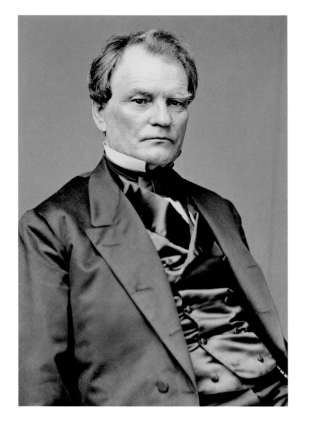

authorities established contraband camps and put blacks to work in support of military operations or laboring in fields to produce cotton for Northern buyers.

Still eager to establish loyal civil regimes that would attract the support of alienated Confederates and other white Southerners, Lincoln announced in December 1863 that he would be willing to pardon former Confederates (excepting high-ranking officials or those people who had betrayed an oath of loyalty to the United States) and that he was willing to support a process of calling new Constitutional Conventions, provided that 10 percent of the 1860 electorate participated in such a process. Those state Conventions would have to abolish slavery; once they provided for new the former Confederate states that would leave the destruction of slavery and the protection of black rights in limbo; they also asserted that former Confederates could not be trusted, while other Republicans held that they should be punished more severely. For the moment, these Republicans argued, the foundations of freedom and loyalty as well as the possibility of black advancement and equality would be best achieved by prolonged Congressional supervision of the process. Other Republicans went further, declaring that the best way to punish former Confederates and break their hold on Southern political, social, and economic life was to confiscate large plantations and distribute the land thus obtained among freedpeople and their families.

Lincoln hesitated. He preferred that the regimes established under his plan would abolish slavery, but he saw the promise of a quick restoration of civil government, not continued federal supervision, as the best way to attract the support of white Southerners. Nor did he have any clear vision of what freedom would look like. He did nothing when William T. Sherman issued Special Field Order No. 15, setting aside lands along the South Carolina coast for use by freedpeople (in part to make sure they ceased following his army as it made its way through the Carolinas). He approved Congress's decision to establish a Bureau of Refugees, Freedmen, and Abandoned Lands (soon known simply as the Freedmen's Bureau) in March 1865 to create a federal role to supervise relief efforts as well as the transition from slavery to freedom as the war drew to a close. Such an agency would be temporary (it did not have its own independent budget), but in its authority to transform confiscated and abandoned lands into 40-acre parcels for use by freedpeople and

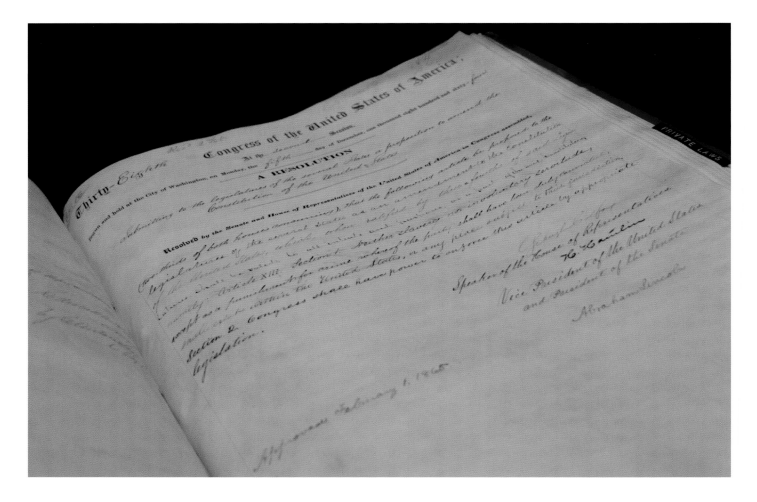

loyal white Southerners, it pointed toward the revolution some Radicals fervently wanted. Black suffrage seemed too much of a reach for federal policy, although in 1864 Lincoln had privately suggested to Louisiana officials that they consider extending the franchise to educated blacks and black veterans. They did not take the hint.

By 1865 there appeared to be little common ground between Lincoln and his Republican opponents on Reconstruction. Although they had come together to support the passage of the Thirteenth Amendment, which, once ratified, would end slavery forever in the United States, they clashed over the fate of Lincoln's plan, with Congress refusing to seat Louisiana's Congressional delegation. However, Lincoln recognized that his measures, framed with wartime priorities in mind, required revision now that there was no need to erode support for the collapsed Confederacy. He

did not yet know what to do next, although, in what proved to be his last public address, on April 11, 1865, he raised as a proposition that perhaps educated blacks and black veterans might be enfranchised. In the audience that evening was the actor John Wilkes Booth, who shuddered at the thought of blacks voting. Three days later, he had his say.

In years to come people would speculate what might have happened during Reconstruction, had Lincoln lived. Such counterfactual contemplations are a far better reflection of the speculator's own assumptions and preferences than they are an insight into what Lincoln might have done, for, as he himself recognized during his last cabinet meeting, held several hours before he departed for Ford's Theater, he did not know what he planned to do. In any case, it would not be left to him to address postwar Reconstruction.

A copy of the Thirteenth Amendment of the United States Constitution held in the Tennessee State Museum.

Andrew Johnson's Reconstruction

Vice President Andrew Johnson had come up the hard way in American politics, winning elections at multiple levels of government, from town alderman and mayor all the way to governor, senator, and vice president. During the secession crisis of 1860–1 he had stood firm for the Union, becoming the only senator from a seceded state to retain his seat in the Senate. Lincoln had appointed him military governor of Tennessee in 1862; in that office he had traveled a long and winding road from pro-slavery advocate to working to secure emancipation in the Volunteer State. Now he was president, and Radical Republicans believed he would act on his pledges to punish traitors.

President Andrew Johnson's vision of reconstruction left the states in charge of determining the rights of African Americans, so long as they accepted the abolition of slavery.

Yet Johnson never viewed Reconstruction as an effort to remake the republic, but merely to restore it. A good Jacksonian Democrat who embraced executive power within a limited federal system, he also harbored deep-seated prejudices against African Americans that remained unshaken in the wake of emancipation. He was eager to restore civil governments throughout the former Confederacy and to leave the fate of the freedpeople in the hands of their former masters and other white Southerners.

By the end of May 1865 Johnson had decided upon a course to pursue. Most white Southerners would be pardoned for their support of the Confederacy if they took an oath of future loyalty. Those who took such an oath would have their ownership of property confirmed (except for slaves), eliminating any notion of widespread confiscation. Excluded from that process were prominent Confederate leaders and people who owned more than $20,000 in taxable property, which included wealthy planters. Those individuals would have to approach Johnson personally to be pardoned. Rather than disrupt the governments formed under Lincoln's plan in Virginia, Louisiana, Arkansas, and his own Tennessee, he let them continue in operation. For the remaining seven former Confederate states, he outlined a process whereby whites not disqualified from participation under his pardon policy would select delegates to state Constitutional Conventions that had to abolish slavery, renounce secession, and void debts financing the Confederate war effort. The process would be supervised by provisional governors appointed by Johnson; they would eventually give way when states held elections under their new constitutions, after which state legislatures would ratify the Thirteenth Amendment. Once Congress seated those states' Congressional delegations, Reconstruction would be complete, at least as far as it concerned the federal government.

Johnson's policy made no provisions for black freedom other than the abolition of slavery. Blacks continued to be excluded from participating in politics as voters and officeholders; nothing was said as to their status as freedpeople under law; Johnson curtailed any discussion of redistributing confiscated lands to the freedpeople by restoring property to anyone who took the oath of allegiance. He left it to white Southerners to determine how to treat black Southerners, and, outside of the operations of the Freedmen's Bureau, he had little to say about how the federal government would facilitate the path from slavery to freedom and beyond.

To be sure, blacks had been working to define what freedom meant for them in the aftermath of the war. Former slaves walked away from plantations, sought to reunite families, embraced opportunities for education, and looked to make a living for themselves and their families. At last, they believed, they had some control over their own lives, so they could move around freely, seek to own their own property, and enjoy their new-

African Americans working on a cotton plantation in South Carolina, 1874. Many ex-slaves had little choice but to work for their former masters.

found freedom. That prospect horrified many whites, who argued that blacks were now insolent, lazy, and had to be coerced to work. Freedom, it seemed, had ruined blacks for white supremacy. However, deprived of their status as property, blacks were now worth nothing to whites: if the violence of slavery had been tempered by the worth of an enslaved worker, that consideration no longer restrained white violence against blacks as human beings. Moreover, as whites retained title to the land they owned, it was left to black agricultural workers to contract with those landowners for planting and harvesting corps. Most blacks had few if any financial resources, and Johnson's policy of restoring land ownership to whites who complied with his pardon policy dissolved the dream of confiscation and redistribution of land to the people who once worked it as plantation slaves.

The Constitutional Conventions and the legislatures elected under their provisions defined black freedom narrowly. There would be no equal protection under law: so-called Black Codes went further and differentiated punishments for various crimes according to the race of the convicted, with blacks receiving sterner consequences. Blacks would not enjoy equal civil rights, including service on juries in cases not involving blacks as parties; it did not take long to learn that civil law enforcement was not interested in protecting blacks from acts of violence committed by whites. Apprenticeship laws allowed whites to force young blacks to work for free under the claim that they were apprentices, and permitted whites to punish their black apprentices.

In the summer and fall of 1865 white Southerners sought to re-establish civil governments upon the foundations of white supremacy and an unapologetic defense of the Confederacy. They protested against the continued presence of black United States soldiers on occupation duty, a consequence of the demobilization of white volunteers and conscripts. Such soldiers protected blacks; their mere existence was an insult to the sensibilities of white supremacists. White Southerners also challenged Johnson's rather lenient terms by calling for compensation for emancipation, refusing to ratify the Thirteenth Amendment, simply rescinding their ordinances of secession, and not repudiating the Confederate war debt. They also elected former Confederates, some of whom had not received a presidential pardon, as governors, congressmen, and senators. Thus, under a president who was sympathetic with many of their concerns, white Southerners had a chance to control what the reconstructed South would look like. Had they, however, gone too far in seeking restoration and the subordination of black Southerners?

Many white Northerners thought so, as did most black Americans. Newspaper reports of unrepentant Southern whites who endeavored to reduce black freedom to the mere absence of legalized slavery led many white Northerners to wonder whether their wartime sacrifices had been in vain. Military authorities sought to protect blacks from intimidation and violence, while Freedmen's Bureau officers addressed reports that white Southern landowners were offering blacks onerous contracts to work their land, only to seek to void those agreements when it came time to pay black workers. Civil courts under Johnson's policy offered blacks little chance of securing justice, leaving the Freedmen's Bureau to intervene and offer protection.

All eyes looked to see where Andrew Johnson stood. Although the president expressed some anxiety over how Southern whites begrudgingly complied with his policy, he parried criticism of its results by claiming that it was merely an experiment that would be reviewed by Congress. However, when Congress convened in December 1865, Republicans refused to seat Congressional delegations elected by white Southerners and commenced framing legislation to protect black rights and blunt the impact of Johnson's policy. Ratification of the Thirteenth Amendment that month might well have ended slavery, but what freedom meant remained undefined, with signs that the president was not interested in pursuing the matter vigorously.

Republicans Respond

Congressional Republicans rejected the consequences of Johnson's policy. If restoration meant the survival of Confederate recalcitrance and the denial of even rough civil equality to blacks, then it must be set aside. Moreover, Republicans knew that with the abolition of slavery the representation of the South in both the House of Representatives and the Electoral College would increase, since now an enslaved person who had counted as 60 percent of a white person would be replaced by a freed black who counted as the same as a white person when it came to determining representation—yet it was evident that the vast majority of white Southerners (and many white Northerners) had no intention of letting blacks vote or hold office.

Republicans formed a Joint Committee on Reconstruction to find out for themselves about conditions in the defeated South. They also began creating legislation to expand the scope of the Freedmen's Bureau and to provide equal protection under law for black civil rights. Finally, they began exploring the need for another Constitutional amendment that would secure the fruits of victory, protect black rights, and address the consequences of the elimination of the three-fifths clause through abolition for purposes of allocating representation and electoral votes. The United States Army, under the direction of General-in-Chief Ulysses S. Grant, also intervened to protect the freedpeople from the impact of the Black Codes and to check white supremacist violence and coercion. However, it was also clear that most Republicans had little stomach for sterner measures, including a prolonged occupation of the South, a significant delay in re-establishing civil governments, or a far-reaching program of confiscation and redistribution of land. The revolution would have to be a legal, institutional, and political one.

Before long Republicans supported two measures that laid the foundation for their endeavors. A new Freedmen's Bureau bill extended the life of the Bureau, provided it with funding, and authorized Bureau agents to interpose themselves in cases where blacks were not being treated equally under the law in Southern states. Building on that premise, the Civil Rights Act of 1866 provided for federal intervention in cases where Southern civil courts failed to offer blacks equal protection under law. It declared that anyone born in the United States (other than Native Americans) was a US citizen with certain rights, including the right to make contracts, to own property, to sue in court, and to enjoy equal protection under law. Beyond this most Republicans were reluctant to go, although the Freedmen's Bureau legislation would have given blacks three more years on lands set aside under Sherman's 1865 order and secured public land for black homesteading and purchase, as did a separate homestead act for the South. Left untouched was confiscation, thus ending hopes of a more fundamental revolution in the Southern social, economic, and political order.

Johnson vetoed both bills, declaring that the Freedmen's Bureau bill provided preferential treatment for the freedpeople while the Civil Rights bill would undermine federalism in favor of a centralized federal government. He took advantage of the occasion of George Washington's birthday to blast Radical Republican leaders in deeply personal terms as disloyal Americans, just like the secessionists. In so doing he burned whatever bridges he might have used to work with Republicans on compromise solutions: he was now convinced that resistance to his policy of toleration

A mural in the Capitol building in Washington D.C. commemorates the passage of the Civil Rights Act of 1866.

A scene from the Memphis Massacre of 1866. It did not take long after the end of the Civil War for white supremacist violence to raise its head.

for former Confederates and white supremacists challenged the Constitution itself. Republicans in Congress failed to overturn Johnson's veto of the Freedmen's Bureau bill, but they succeeded in overriding the veto of the Civil Rights Act; a second Freedmen's Bureau bill several months later (also passed over a Johnson veto) that treated the issue of land for the freedmen in far more limited terms while providing for military commissions to address issues of injustice against blacks would fare better.

Johnson's vetoes redoubled Republican efforts to frame a new amendment to the Constitution, in part because an amendment was not subject to presidential veto. The proposed Fourteenth Amendment defined US citizenship in terms of civil rights and equality before the law; it declared that any effort to deny citizens the right to vote because of race or color would result in reducing a state's representation in Congress (and thus its strength in the Electoral College) accordingly; it repudiated the Confederate war debt; and it barred

former Confederates who had violated an oath of loyalty to the United States from holding office or serving in the military unless Congress repealed that prohibition. As soon as the amendment made its way to the states for ratification, Tennessee, with Johnson's arch-enemy William G. Brownlow serving as governor, ratified the measure, and Congress seated its Congressional delegation.

That something had to be done to address affairs in the South, especially white supremacist violence and terrorism, was increasingly evident. In May 1866 whites in Memphis attacked blacks, including recently discharged US veterans, killing 46 blacks and destroying black homes, churches, and schools. Two months later, when a group of Louisiana Republicans sought to reconvene the state's Constitutional Convention to pass measures to contain the political re-emergence of former Confederates, white supremacists and policemen joined in attacking delegates (only 25 showed up) and their supporters as they marched through the streets of New Orleans.

The violence in Memphis, New Orleans, and elsewhere shocked many Northerners and convinced Republicans to press forward with their plans for Reconstruction. Johnson had a different plan in mind. He sought to reconstitute the National Union party—the formal name the Republicans had adopted for the 1864 presidential election—as an alliance of white conservatives, conservative Republicans, and Northern Democrats with the goal of battling Republicans during the 1866 midterm elections. In support of this enterprise, Johnson undertook a speaking tour throughout much of the North, ostensibly to dedicate a statue of Stephen Douglas in Chicago. Along for the journey under some duress were Grant, recently elevated to the rank of four-star general of the army, Admiral David G. Farragut

of "damn the torpedoes" fame at Mobile Bay, and assorted cabinet members and minor luminaries. Although the trip began uneventfully enough, as the president's train made its way west across New York towards Ohio and Indiana, making many stops along the way, Johnson exchanged taunts with hecklers who cued their outbursts in response to the Tennessean's standard stump speech. The president suggested that some of his enemies be hanged, compared himself to Jesus Christ, and even hinted that Providence had arranged for Lincoln's death to allow Johnson to become president. Every comment, the more outrageous the better, was faithfully reported by the press, although Johnson never grasped how he had humiliated himself. What became known as the "Swing Around the Circle" proved to be a

A cartoon from 1866 critical of Andrew Johnson and his disastrous "Swing Around the Circle" campaign.

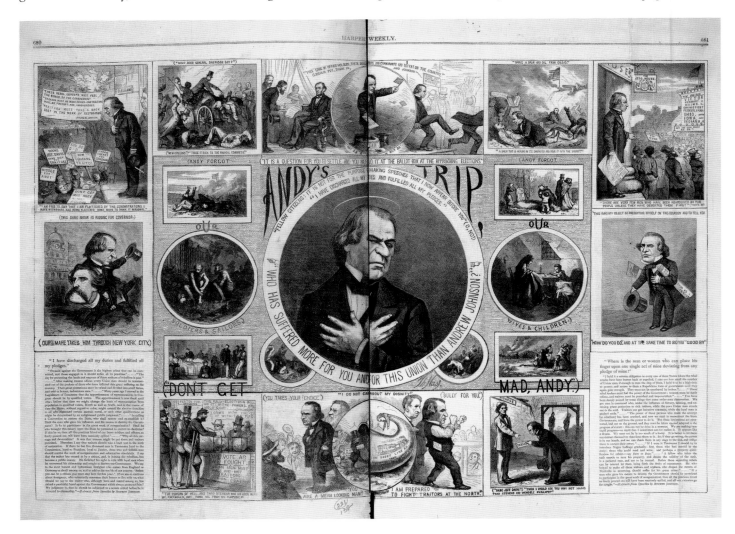

Edwin M. Stanton, Secretary of War from 1862 until 1868, was a bitter opponent of Andrew Johnson. He had been appointed by Lincoln, and when Johnson attempted to remove him from office, he refused to resign.

self-inflicted wound on the president's political prospects; Grant remarked that he was "disgusted at hearing a man make speeches on the way to his own funeral." More alarming were reports that Johnson was considering organizing a Congress loyal to him and using the army to dissolve the present Congress. When Grant firmly opposed that idea, the president contemplated sending him to Mexico on a diplomatic mission to get him out of the way. The fall elections proved a Republican triumph that secured veto-proof majorities in both houses of Congress. The reports of anti-black violence in the South presaged a resurgent Confederacy; it was time to counter such rebellious behavior by ratifying the Fourteenth Amendment, endorsing Congressional measures, and undoing Johnson's failed initiative intended to restore civil government founded on white supremacist principles, all the while containing the behavior of a seemingly emotionally imbalanced president.

Republican Reconstruction, Impeachment, and the Election of 1868

In the wake of the election of 1866, Republicans, emboldened by having a veto-proof majority in both houses of Congress, decided to impose their own plan for restoring civil governments throughout the 10 remaining states that refused to ratify the Fourteenth Amendment. They crafted legislation which provided for new state Constitutional Conventions that would undo the handiwork of Johnson's policy. While some former Confederates would not take part in the selection of delegates for these Conventions, African American males would for the first time cast ballots in large numbers and be eligible to serve as delegates. The first Reconstruction Act divided the 10 remaining former Confederate states into five military districts, each headed by a general appointed by the president to oversee the process. The Conventions would frame new state constitutions that would establish suffrage for all United States citizens, regardless of race, and provide for state elections. Once these elections took place, and the resulting state legislatures ratified the Fourteenth Amendment, Congress would seat their Congressional delegations and restore civil rule.

Nor was this all. Aware of the need to handcuff Johnson in his attempts to thwart the implementation of this policy, Congress also passed the Tenure of Office Act, which stated that the president could not remove from office any federal official whose appointment required Senate confirmation. Should Congress be out of session, the president might suspend an officeholder covered by the legislation, appoint a temporary replacement, and then await the Senate's decision on the removal. Whether this act protected cabinet officers appointed by Lincoln, including Johnson's foe, Secretary of War Edwin M. Stanton, from unilateral removal by Johnson was not clear. A rider attached to an appropriations bill provided that all orders issued by the president to military personnel had to go through the general-in-chief, who was authorized to establish his headquarters wherever he desired. Republicans designed the measure to insulate Grant from Johnson's machinations and to prevent any talk of the president using the army to counter Congress. Violations of either law were defined as among the "high crimes and misdemeanors" that would leave the president liable to impeachment and removal.

The Reconstruction Act and the Tenure of Office Act survived a presidential veto and became law on March 2, 1867, while Johnson reluctantly signed the appropriations act that included the provision to protect Grant. But the Reconstruction Acts were far from perfect. Three weeks later Congress passed, over presidential veto, a second act outlining the registration process and how the state Constitutional Conventions would operate. Johnson and Attorney General Henry Stanbury battled Grant over how to interpret the legislation and the president tried to obstruct the registration process. Congress passed a third Reconstruction Act in July, enhancing the power of district commanders and Grant. It then chose to adjourn for the summer, ignoring Grant's warning that, once Congress was not in session, Johnson would escalate his obstructionism.

Grant was right. No sooner had Congress adjourned than Johnson suspended Stanton after the secretary declined to resign. The president appointed Grant to act as secretary of war, and Grant accepted in order to prevent Johnson from naming someone who might thwart Congressional intent. The president then removed several district commanders who were vigorous in their support of Congress's policy, including war hero Philip H. Sheridan. Grant's protest against these removals proved unavailing: Congress had erred by failing to protect them, while as military officers they were still subject to Johnson's orders. The result pitted the president against the general-in-chief in a struggle that had political as well as institutional implications.

Johnson soon scored another victory during the elections of 1867, which would determine which party controlled several key Northern states, including the state legislatures that elected senators. In several states Republicans advocated suffrage for their states' blacks, allowing Democrats to play upon Northern racism as they argued that it was time to put an end to radical changes in the Northern polity. The result proved costly to Republicans. In Ohio, for example, while Republican gubernatorial candidate Rutherford B. Hayes squeaked through to victory, Democrats took control of the state legislature, thus dooming Radical Republican Senator Benjamin F. Wade's bid for re-election. The lesson was clear: Republicans would fare better at the polls throughout the North if they claimed that Democratic triumphs would mean endangering the fruits of victory from the war while refraining from advocating political equality for African Americans throughout the nation. The results also implied that Republicans needed to select a presidential candidate in 1868 who was not linked to the radical wing of the party while standing as a symbol of Union triumph. The obvious choice was Ulysses S. Grant. Could Republicans overcome Grant's disdain of politics by arguing that his candidacy would preserve in peace what had been secured through war?

Emboldened by Democratic triumphs, Johnson chose to escalate his battle with Congressional Republicans. At first he sought to enlist Grant in support of his effort to resist the Senate's restoration of Stanton to the cabinet, but the general refused to cooperate, and the two men had a public falling out which reassured wary Republicans that Grant was on their side. Johnson then attempted to fire Stanton outright in defiance of the Tenure of Office Act, leading the House of Representatives to impeach him on February 24, 1868. It would be left to the Republican-dominated Senate whether to convict and oust the Tennessean from office.

As the impeachment crisis reached a boil, in the South military authorities supervised the registration of voters who would elect delegates to state Constitutional Conventions in compliance with the legislation. For the first time significant numbers of African Americans would be part of the political process as voters and delegates. Many of them joined Union Leagues, which had originated as organizations for upper-class urban Northern whites but were now instruments of black political mobilization. The handiwork of these conventions included provisions for equal treatment and protection under law, the establishment of a public

The conflict between the Democratic President Andrew Johnson and the Republican Congress came to a head in 1868, when Congress impeached Johnson for his violation of the recently passed Tenure of Office Act.

HARPER'S WEEKLY.
A JOURNAL OF CIVILIZATION.

VOL. XI.—No. 568.]   NEW YORK, SATURDAY, NOVEMBER 16, 1867.   [SINGLE COPIES TEN CENTS.
[$4.00 PER YEAR IN ADVANCE.

Entered according to Act of Congress, in the Year 1867, by Harper & Brothers, in the Clerk's Office of the District Court for the Southern District of New York.

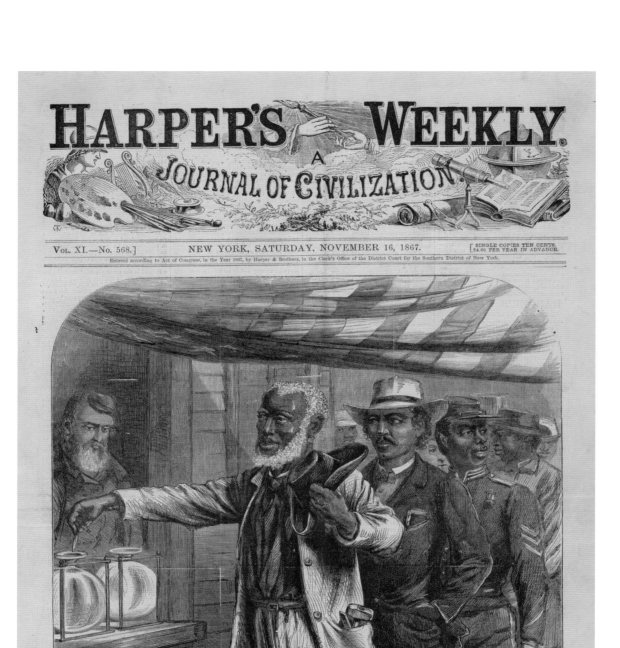

"THE FIRST VOTE."—Drawn by A. R. Waud.—[See next Page.]

An African American casts his vote in 1867 in the first opportunity for the newly enfranchised to participate in elections.

education system, revised taxation structures, and the reform of political institutions to make them more democratic. Delegates embraced expanding public institutions, including prisons, asylums for people unable to take care of themselves (including orphans), and in some instances relief for the poor and impoverished. They also worked to create a state government that would support economic development and public investment or assistance for such endeavors as well as debt relief on a more limited scale; efforts at creating opportunities for blacks to secure land proved less successful. In many cases, these conventions minimized Confederate disenfranchisement as evidence of their commitment to an inclusive democratic order (at least for men). Whites, both Northern-born and native Southerners, as well as blacks who had been free or enslaved, were part of the Republican coalition that saw these visions realized in Constitutional prose.

That these Conventions met at all was something of a miracle, given the resistance of many white Southerners. Some refused to register or vote, requiring Congress to modify the terms of their process lest non-participation lead to a failure to secure a majority of the state's eligible voters as required by the earlier Reconstruction Acts. Others resorted to violence and intimidation, embodied in the rise of the most famous of white supremacist terrorist groups, the Ku Klux Klan, which had first become visible in 1866 as resistance to black equality and Republican rule mounted throughout the South. Thus, as states conducted elections under the new constitutions, and newly formed state legislatures ratified the Fourteenth Amendment, Republicans found themselves the targets of terrorism designed to intimidate and eliminate supporters of Reconstruction, white as well as black. In Georgia such forces actually succeeded in transforming the state legislature into a Democratic majority by insisting that the new constitution did not provide for black officeholders.

As Southern states crafted new constitutions, Andrew Johnson fought for political survival. Although several of the articles of impeachment

addressed Johnson's behavior as president, most of them focused on whether he had violated the Tenure of Office Act. Given that it was unclear as to whether Stanton was covered under the legislation's provisions, the debate became one of politics, not law. Aware that, should Johnson be removed from office, Wade would succeed him, several moderate Republicans wondered whether Wade's radicalism when it came to race and his interest in supporting inflationary policies might damage the party's chances in the 1868 presidential contest. Johnson's representatives leaked assurances that the president would tone down his resistance to Reconstruction. This proved sufficient: Johnson

NATIONAL UNION
REPUBLICAN NOMINATION

FOR PRESIDENT,

Gen. U. S. GRANT

FOR VICE PRESIDENT,

SCHUYLER COLFAX

The Republicans nominated Ulysses S. Grant as their presidential candidate. He would take a much more radical approach to reconstruction than Johnson ever had.

Horatio Seymour, the former governor of New York, obtained the Democratic Party nomination in 1868 after a long and convoluted convention in which there was no clear front-runner.

survived by a single vote. Republicans looked to more traditional means of securing the presidency, and within weeks nominated Grant for president at their convention in Chicago. Meeting in New York that July, Democrats decided to make the war, race, and reconstruction the central issues of the fall contest when they finally chose former New York governor Horatio Seymour as their candidate. That Seymour had once addressed mobs targeting blacks during the 1863 New York City Draft Riots as "my friends" offered one clear indication of his sentiments, as did the pledge made by his running mate, Frank P. Blair Jr. of Missouri, that a Seymour administration would undo Republican Reconstruction.

Such extreme rhetoric allowed Republicans to embrace a campaign that refought the war once more. They successfully linked Democrats with former Confederates, including white supremacist terrorists such as former Confederate general Nathan Bedford Forrest, recognized by many as the leader of the Ku Klux Klan. They downplayed black equality and black suffrage; they celebrated Grant's military accomplishments. For his part, Grant reluctantly accepted his political fate, believing that politicians from both parties were bent on destroying what military victory seemed to achieve. His simple utterance upon accepting the nomination, "Let us have peace," promised an end to strife, chaos, upheaval, and distraction. More popular than the party that had nominated him, Grant looked to secure the fruits of Union victory one more time at the polls.

Grant triumphed, but a closer look at the outcome revealed much about Republican Reconstruction. Had only whites voted, he would still have secured a victory in the electoral college due to winning Northern states with more electoral votes. What gave Grant his margin in the popular vote and enabled him to carry six of the eight former Confederate states in the contest was the votes of African Americans

who cast their first presidential ballot. Over the summer, eight Southern states, having ratified the Fourteenth Amendment and complied with the Reconstruction Acts, saw Republicans in Congress seat their delegations and render them eligible to participate in the fall contest. If Republicans wanted a national party, they would have to protect blacks from violence and fraud, even if that eroded the party's strength in the North; should that margin become imperiled, Republicans might find themselves compelled to abandon their efforts in the South to shore up their chances in the North, becoming a regional party yet again.

The inauguration of Ulysses S. Grant as president on March 4, 1869.

CHAPTER 10
RECONSTRUCTION UNDER GRANT

ULYSSES S. GRANT'S TRIUMPH in the 1868 presidential contest promised an end to Reconstruction on terms favorable to Republicans, or so it seemed at the time. Yet within eight years, the combined impact of Northern weariness, resilient and recalcitrant white Southerners, charges of corruption, limited federal power, and economic depression wore away at such bright prospects. Grant had done much to save the Union and to destroy slavery, but he came up short in his efforts to protect black equality and opportunity. It is unlikely that anyone else who could have secured the presidency would have done better, but that was poor consolation to the freedpeople.

Grant's First Term

No sooner had Grant won than Republicans revisited their efforts to secure suffrage for blacks in the North, a matter of political pragmatism as well as principle given the resurgence in Democrat strength in closely-contested Northern states. Aware that attempting to achieve change state-by-state had been politically costly, they chose instead to pursue the ratification of a Constitutional amendment, a process not subject to popular vote and where their control of state legislatures, North as well as South, would prove crucial. The amendment forbade states from refusing the right to vote to American citizens on the grounds of "race, color, or previous condition of servitude," and authorized Congress to enforce the act by appropriate legislation. Upon taking the oath of office on March 4, 1869, Grant endorsed the amendment, hoping that it would bring an end to the controversy over black suffrage.

At the time of Grant's inauguration, three states—Virginia, Mississippi, and Texas—had failed to complete the process laid out in the Reconstruction Acts. White Virginians, for example, complained that the disenfranchisement of former Confederates under the proposed state constitution was too harsh a penalty. Grant facilitated a compromise whereby voters would vote on that clause separately from the remainder of the new constitution; the measure failed while the constitution was ratified, and Virginia completed the process. However, the president rejected a similar course in Mississippi, and Republicans prevailed, as they did in Texas. Meanwhile, he supported the remanding of Georgia to military supervision following the rampant violence that had characterized that state's politics in 1868. Still, by 1870 Georgia completed the process as well, meaning that civil rule had been restored throughout the nation. By that time the Fifteenth Amendment had been ratified, with Grant working for its adoption. But Reconstruction did not end in 1870, in large part because white Southern Democrats were willing to use violence and intimidation to regain power in their region.

An 1870 print celebrating the passage of the Fifteenth Amendment.

Grant sought another solution that he hoped would give Southern blacks some economic leverage. In 1869 agents of the Dominican Republic suggested that it might welcome being annexed by the United States. Grant, believing that such an acquisition would serve American strategic and economic interests, pursued negotiations. Privately he reasoned that if Southern blacks threatened to emigrate to the Dominican Republic, white Southerners might be forced to treat blacks as citizens and voters lest they lose a critical portion of their labor force. However, the proposal proved controversial, and the ensuing debate over annexation pitted Grant against Senator Charles Sumner of Massachusetts and Senator Carl Schurz of Missouri, among others, who began to work against Grant's renomination. The bitter infighting among Republicans complicated finding solutions to protect black and white Southern Republicans; at the same time it soon became evident that many Republicans were beginning to lose interest in Reconstruction, with several party leaders complaining that the federal government had already done all it could on behalf of protecting Southern blacks without violating the principles of federalism and limited centralized power.

Southern Republicanism

In the Southern states, Republican governments battled to survive and build viable majorities in the face of great adversity. In states where a majority of the electorate was African American, the challenge was deceptively simple: make sure those voters, the vast majority of whom would cast ballots for Republican candidates, could vote safely. In states

Grant hoped to annex the Dominican Republic, which he believed could force the South to recognize African American civil rights.

where a majority of the electorate was white, Republicans worked to attract and retain the support of those white Southerners who were attracted by the party's message of state-supported economic development more than a commitment to protecting the achievements of emancipation. Both approaches confronted the challenge of white supremacist terrorist violence aimed at overthrowing Republican rule; complicating that difficult task was the realization that requests for federal intervention would raise the cry of "bayonet rule!" and call into question the ability of these governments to sustain themselves as well as their legitimacy.

Across the South, Republicans promoted government support of economic development, including issuing bonds to build railroads. They also supported public education for all, although usually in segregated schools. The promise of prosperity was one way to try to woo white Southerners to vote Republican; at the same time blacks were an integral part of the electorate as well as the legislative process, with blacks serving in the state legislatures while several rose to sit in Congress as senators or representatives. Critics of these governments charged that they were exercises in corruption. To be sure, there were some instances where Southern Republicans engaged in corrupt activities, but the same was true of American political leaders elsewhere, such as New York City's Democrats under William M. Tweed, leader of the infamous Tweed Ring. On the whole, Republican state governments in the South were no more or less corrupt than the Democratic regimes that eventually succeeded them, but Reconstruction's opponents made much of the issue, with vivid portrayals of venal carpetbaggers from the North, opportunistic white Southern scalawags, and incompetent and ignorant blacks joining together to line their pockets at the expense of the majority of white

The ruins of Atlanta's railroad roundhouse in 1866. Southern Republicans emphasized the need for economic regeneration, particularly through the railroads.

Southerners (read former Confederates who were members of the Democratic party).

Despite the achievements of these state governments, Democrats remained determined to overthrow them. Virginia nearly managed to avoid Republican rule altogether, as a conservative Republican governor eventually gave way relatively peacefully to Democratic supremacy, with Republicans remaining competitive in state and national elections during Grant's presidency. In Tennessee, North Carolina, and Georgia, violence played a larger role in unseating Republican governors and state legislatures, with the Ku Klux Klan and other paramilitary terrorist organizations claiming victory. Although in some states, such as Arkansas, Republicans fought back at the state level, all too often they preferred to seek federal intervention, arguing that to raise a biracial state militia to defend their regimes would simply intensify conflict. Also damaging Republican efforts at retaining power were emerging divisions within several state Republican organizations—sometimes over how best to attract support and establish legitimacy, sometimes the result of simple clashes between ambitious rivals. In either case political conflict often transformed into bitter struggles for survival, with violence and intimidation at the core of the tactics of white supremacist Democrats.

Republicans Strike Back

In several Southern states, Southern Republicans sought to defend themselves, and at times achieved momentary successes. However, these triumphs were often short-lived. While Republicans battled back in Arkansas, in North Carolina they were overwhelmed in what eventually resembled violence that was little short of war. If Southern Republicans were to survive, they needed assistance from the federal government.

Republicans first sought to address the need to enforce the law through the expansion of the federal government's ability to arrest, try, and convict terrorists through the creation of the

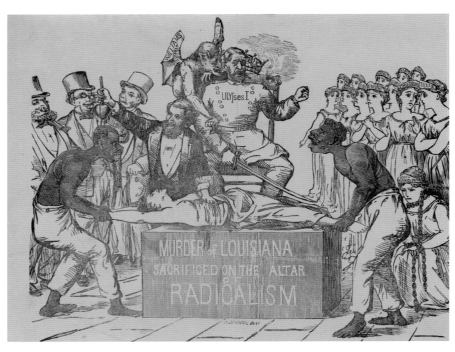

Department of Justice in 1869; however, the department never received support sufficient to pursue its mission in a time of fiscal restraint and concern about too much federal power. Congress commenced passing legislation to arm the federal government with the legal justification to protect black voters from violence and intimidation. A series of Enforcement Acts authorized federal supervision of federal elections and provided for federal intervention should states prove unable or unwilling to provide such protection, empowering the president to use force when necessary to protect the right to vote as provided for by the Fifteenth Amendment. The most powerful of these acts, also known as the Ku Klux Act, became law in 1871. It authorized the president to suspend the privilege of the writ of habeas corpus and declare martial law where warranted and to order federal military forces to put down violence. However, these powers were so extraordinary to the legislation's framers that they limited the exercise of such power throughout the next session of Congress.

President Grant decided to target South Carolina, where violence threatened to thwart the will of the state's black majority to support Republican candidates. In the fall of 1871, he invoked the Ku Klux Act to break up terrorism

A cartoon lampoons the election of the carpetbagger William P. Kellogg to the governorship of Louisiana, while Ulysses S. Grant turns a blind eye.

and bring terrorists to justice. In the short term, he succeeded, cracking the back of the Ku Klux Klan in South Carolina and elsewhere, but the triumph proved short-lived. The federal government's effectiveness at subduing terrorism led the terrorists to seek more sophisticated ways of prevailing that minimized the chance of triggering federal intervention, while the federal government did not always prosecute the cases before it due to inadequate resources and at times questionable commitment.

Reelecting Grant

By the end of 1871, Republicans unhappy with Grant's performance as president concluded that they could do nothing to block his renomination. While some Republican notables reluctantly accepted that conclusion, others set in motion a proposal for a new party which would soon be labeled the Liberal Republican movement. Among its leaders were Senator Carl Schurz of Missouri,

who had clashed with the administration multiple times, and a number of newspaper editors, led by Horace Greeley of the *New York Tribune*. They found support in various intellectuals who embraced widespread but somewhat ill-defined calls for reform, including Henry Adams, a member of the fourth generation of a family of presidents, diplomats, and public servants, who edited the *North American Review*, and Edwin L. Godkin, who headed *The Nation*, a journal of political opinion. It was a movement of disgruntled political and intellectual elites seeking support to capture power. It also represented a realization that the original Republican party had fulfilled its goals of saving the Union and destroying slavery, leaving its members to discover that on other issues there was little common ground.

The new party struggled to find coherence beyond dissatisfaction with Grant. Some of its leaders pushed for civil service reform, free trade, and an end to Reconstruction, while other

A Ku Klux Klan attack in the 1870s. In the early parts of the decade, increasing white terror in the South required a stronger federal response. Grant empowered the authorities through the Ku Klux Act of 1871.

dissenting Republicans flocked to the movement because they had found themselves on the outside of power in Washington. This menagerie of unhappy politicians and editors gathered at Cincinnati in May 1872 to nominate a candidate, with Greeley emerging as the party's standard bearer. Given that Greeley's mercurial political career had included taking stands at odds with the party's cries for reform, it was difficult to argue with the notion that the party's slogan was a declaration Schurz deplored: "Anything to beat Grant!" Democrats, struggling to regain ground nationally, adopted Greeley as their own candidate.

Grant had already taken steps to blunt criticism of his administration. In 1871 he had called for civil service reform, depriving his foes of one of their chief issues. Although Southern politics still showed signs of contention and violence, for a while it looked as if Grant's willingness to meet white Southerners halfway while protecting black rights and subduing the Ku Klux Klan was moving the nation closer to a just, stable, and lasting reunion. The administration could also brag that its foreign policy had brought about the peaceful settlement of outstanding issues with Great Britain arising out of the war. The Treaty of Washington (1871) provided for a mediated arbitration process, which took place in Geneva, Switzerland, in 1872, with the United States emerging satisfied with the outcome. It appeared that peace and prosperity were to be Grant's hallmarks, while his early missteps faded from public memory.

Having secured firm control of the party, Grant easily won renomination. Regular Republicans rallied behind the savior of the Union who sought to preserve in peace what he had won in war. They successfully linked Greeley with Democratic support for the Confederacy and white supremacy while dismissing dissident Republicans as soreheads whose ambitions had been thwarted because Grant did not share their high opinion of themselves. Once more Grant appeared as the candidate of stability and progress, while Greeley struggled to articulate a message beyond criticism of the incumbent as an incompetent drunken military despot (or the puppet of various Republican regulars), various charges of corruption, and reconciliation with the white South while claiming that all that had been promised black Americans had been delivered to them. However, cartoonist Thomas Nast's relentless pursuit of Greeley in the pages of *Harper's Weekly* ensured that voters saw Grant's foe as slightly ridiculous.

Grant easily claimed victory on election day. Greeley died soon afterwards, and the Liberal Republican movement disintegrated, with many of its participants sullenly rejoining the ranks of regular Republicans, their opposition to Grant notwithstanding. Although terrorist tactics suppressed Southern Republican support, Grant still managed to carry six of the former Confederate states, while in two others (Louisiana and Arkansas) the returns were so disputed that the Senate declined to count their electoral votes. However, the results suggested that the political situation in the South had not yet stabilized, while Republican observers noted that Grant could have retained the White House without winning a single former Confederate state. The president viewed the triumph as the voters' vindication of his course. It would not be too long, however, before he and his fellow Republicans would find themselves under fire once more, and not just because of affairs in the South.

Grant's Second Term

During the campaign of 1872 investigative reporters uncovered a scheme to bribe members of Congress in the 1860s during the construction of the transcontinental railroad. A construction company for the Union Pacific Railroad erected a shell organization, known as Credit Mobilier, that distributed stock to members of Congress in the hopes that such members would be so favorably disposed toward the endeavor to build the railroads that they would not scrutinize the use of federal funds to assist in it, thus allowing investors to reap large profits. In the aftermath of the election, Congress investigated its own members, and learned that several of them, including outgoing vice president Schuyler Colfax, incoming vice president Henry Wilson, and several members of Congress, the most prominent of whom was Ohio Republican congressman James A. Garfield, had been tainted by accepting stock on credit. Although the scandal occurred during Andrew Johnson's administration, the revelations darkened the Grant administration just as it embarked on its second term, as did an effort by Congress to offer itself a retroactive pay raise, an event soon labeled the Salary Grab.

Nor did white terrorism entirely subside. In several Southern states, there were disputes as to which party had prevailed in 1872, with violence escalating most visibly in Louisiana. On April 13, 1873, upwards of one hundred African Americans were slaughtered in cold blood at Colfax, Louisiana, as Democrats sought to regain control of the state. Efforts to prosecute the perpetrators

African Americans gather their dead and wounded after the violence of the Colfax Massacre in Louisiana on April 13, 1873.

WEALTH.
Compiled from 9th Census.

Even before the Panic of 1873 the distribution of wealth in the United States was widely unequal, as this map based on the census one year earlier demonstrates.

the president's decision to veto a bill providing for a moderate inflation of the currency won plaudits as a resounding defense of the nation's credit, people in debt chafed at the failure to help them in their time of need.

Already shouldering the burdens of these shortcomings, Grant endeavoured to protect remaining Southern Republican governments from being overthrown by violence, especially in Louisiana, where Democrats nearly overthrew the Republican governor in September 1874. Southern Republicans struggled to survive, as Democrats exploited their opportunities to regain power in several states. Democrats claimed victory in the midterm elections of 1874, regaining control of the House of Representatives for the first time since the war. This enabled them to block any further Reconstruction legislation and to launch investigations of the Grant administration, in the course of which they found plenty of opportunities to question the probity of administration officials. Grant defended his administration's support of Reconstruction: "Treat the negro as a citizen and a voter—as he is and must remain—and soon parties will be divided, not on the color line, but on principle. Then we shall have no complaint of sectional interference." In January 1875 Louisiana Democrats tried once more to seize control of their state government,

The New York Stock Exchange closes its doors on September 20, 1873 as a global recession began with the so-called "Panic of 1873."

of the massacre soon ran afoul of a federal court ruling in *US v. Cruikshank, et al.*, which narrowly interpreted the Enforcement Acts, thus depriving them of much of their effectiveness.

Just as crippling to Republican Reconstruction was the Panic of 1873, in which an overextension of credit, followed by its inevitable contraction, led to a global economic downturn that manifested itself as a serious depression in the United States. In the South, efforts to build railroads as the best evidence of Republicans' efforts to attract Southern whites collapsed; Democrats blamed Republicans for the disaster, and struggling Southern whites rebelled against the notion of paying increased taxes to support such state activities as public education, which benefited African Americans. In the North, Democrats targeted Republicans, saying that the nation could not afford to spend money on Reconstruction initiatives while neglecting white Northerners' economic concerns. As if Credit Mobilier, the Salary Grab, and the Panic of 1873 were not enough to cripple Republican political prospects as the midterm elections of 1874 approached, rumors that Grant might seek a third term raised the prospect that the general turned president might be seeking a dictatorship. While

only to be thwarted by federal troops, who broke up an effort to organize the state legislature to serve Democratic ends. Such federal intervention came under heavy criticism from Reconstruction's opponents across the nation, who attempted to portray the appearance of federal soldiers in a legislative chamber as portending military rule. In a strongly worded message, Grant defended his administration's actions while assailing his critics. Referring to the Colfax massacre, he declared, "Fierce denunciations ring through the country about office holding and election matters in Louisiana, while every one of the Colfax miscreants goes unwhipped of justice, and no way can be found in this boasted land of civilization and Christianity to punish the perpetrators of this bloody and monstrous Crime."

Grant's powerful address momentarily checked criticism of his administration's policies, but by the spring of 1875 only four Southern states—Mississippi, South Carolina, Louisiana, and Florida—remained under Republican rule. Court decisions and the Democratic majority in the House of Representatives crippled enforcement efforts, while wavering public support for intervention in a time of economic depression pointed to Reconstruction as becoming politically untenable for Republicans. This became evident

that September in Mississippi, where Democrats embraced a strategy known as the Mississippi Plan, which pledged to regain power "peaceably if we can, and forcibly if we must." When Republican governor Adelbert Ames requested federal intervention, Grant hesitated, aware that Republican leaders were warning him that to intervene in Mississippi might spell disaster for party fortunes in the critical state of Ohio. Mississippi Democrats played their hand well. Once Ohio voters had cast their ballots in October, with the Republicans narrowly claiming victory and Rutherford B. Hayes securing the governorship, Mississippi Democrats negotiated a ceasefire with Ames, thus avoiding federal intervention—and then abandoned the deal with the election a few days away, long before federal force could make its impact felt. Democrats prevailed in Mississippi; Republicans revisited their approach to winning elections, wondering whether Reconstruction had become an albatross around the party's neck.

Republicans were barely clinging to power in South Carolina, Louisiana, and Florida as 1876 began. Grant's administration was rocked by a series of scandals, including an investigation of the so-called Whiskey Ring—an attempt to defraud the federal government of revenue from excise taxes on alcohol—that reached all the way to Grant's private secretary, Orville E. Babcock. That Grant himself had authorized Secretary of the Treasury Benjamin H. Bristow to conduct the investigation did not relieve him of its stigma, while the resignation of his secretary of war in the wake of revelations that implicated him in the sale of post traderships in the west made things worse. In the nation's centennial celebration of its declaring independence, Republicans struggled to nominate Grant's successor, finally settling on none other that Rutherford B. Hayes, who was not closely associated with the president and who had a reputation as a reformer. So did his Democratic opponent, former New York governor Samuel J. Tilden, who had prevailed over New York City's Tweed Ring. Although Democrats in South Carolina stumbled when they went after African Americans at Hamburg in July, on the whole they proved much more skillful in their use of violence and intimidation, while hoping that enough Northern voters were so tired of Republican rule that they would decide to give the Democrats a chance.

A Disputed Election

On election night 1876, it looked as if Tilden and the Democrats would prevail. Before long, however, it was evident that the returns in the three Southern states with Republican governors—Louisiana, South Carolina, and Florida—were contested, along with questions about the qualifications of a single elector in Oregon. Tilden's 184 electoral votes fell one shy of the number he needed to win; if Hayes could capture all 20 disputed electoral votes, he would be Grant's successor. White Southerners and some Democrats muttered darkly about using force to secure the presidency; Grant indicated that he would stop any such effort in its tracks. Had all eligible voters been allowed to cast ballots, of course, Hayes would have won—it was the suppression of Southern Republican votes that brought Tilden close to the victory Democrats so dearly sought. Instead, Southern Republican-controlled returning boards, using means fair and foul, undid what Democrats had achieved through violence and intimidation.

Votes are counted in the disputed presidential election of 1876.

David M. Key, the Senator for Tennessee and a Southern Democrat, was appointed as postmaster general as a part of the Compromise of 1877.

Republicans and Democrats deadlocked over exactly how to determine which set of returns would be recognized as legitimate. Finally, members of Congress from both houses, encouraged by Grant, hammered out a process that established an electoral commission to decide upon disputed returns, with the proviso that both houses could vote to overturn the commission's ruling. The composition of the commission reflected its inherently political nature: of its 15 members, five came from the Senate (three Republicans, two Democrats), five from the House (three Democrats, two Republicans), and the final five from the Supreme Court. Initially two Republican and two Democratic justices would be joined by Independent David Davis of Illinois, but Davis resigned his position on the Court when Democrats in Illinois secured his election to the Senate. Democrats, believing that Davis would side with them (he later suggested that might not have been the case), settled for Joseph P. Bradley, a Grant appointee from New Jersey who had ruled against the administration in several key Reconstruction cases.

It did not take long to discover that, beneath the veneer of institutional justice and objectivity, the commission's members would follow their partisan preferences—a conclusion that held as true for the Democrats as it did for the Republicans. Thus, on every critical vote, the Republicans prevailed, meaning that over time all 20 disputed electoral votes were counted for Hayes. However, these triumphs did not secure the futures of Republican governors in Florida, Louisiana, or South Carolina: Florida slipped into Democratic hands as soon as the Electoral Commission concluded considering its case, while Grant confided his willingness to allow the same to happen in Louisiana. But Southern Democrats were willing to block the completion of the process by filibustering if they failed to extract concessions from Republicans. These included the abandonment of the Republican governments in Louisiana and South Carolina, the appointment of a Southern Democrat to the cabinet, and Republican support for legislation to rebuild Southern infrastructure such as levees along the southern Mississippi and a southern transcontinental railroad. To facilitate that goal, they claimed they were willing to help elect a Republican speaker of the House.

Much has been made of this so-called Compromise of 1877, but key aspects of the alleged bargain did not represent substantial concessions, and other understandings never materialized as legislation. Hayes had already decided to embark on a different approach in Southern policy that doomed the remaining Republican state regimes, and was quite willing to foster sectional reconciliation (and build white support for a revamped Republican party) by appointing a white Southerner to the cabinet (Tennessee's David M. Key became postmaster general). The rumored economic legislation never came into being, and Democrats elected one of their own speaker of the house. Republicans realized that if they recovered their strength in the North as the economy rebounded they could rid themselves of Reconstruction, which was increasingly becoming an albatross around the party's neck. This meant that African Americans, especially in the South, would increasingly be left to fend for themselves as Democratic-controlled state governments narrowed what freedom meant by statute, practice, and legislation, but not all white Republicans seriously regretted that outcome.

Reconstruction was over. A majority of white Americans chose sectional reconciliation, however begrudgingly, over the protection of black rights and opportunities as the price one had to pay to move on. It would be left to future generations to endeavor to realize its unfulfilled promise. For now, a war that had preserved the Union, destroyed slavery, and established the constitutional foundation for future change was enough, even if it was far from enough for black Americans.

The Soldiers' National Monument at Gettysburg was completed in 1869. Ever since the war ended, memorials to the soldiers who lost their lives in it have dotted the American landscape.

CONCLUSION
THE CIVIL WAR
REMEMBERED

MOST AMERICANS CLAIM to be aware of their past, whereas in truth they have rarely paused to gain a discerning understanding of it. To be sure, they may visit historical sites, motor around battlefields, and perhaps consume a good deal of literature about history or watch movies and television programs devoted to retelling tales of the past, but as often as not their comprehension of the people and events of American history is superficial and sometimes badly misinformed. A good number of people who declare a passion for history pursue it as they would rooting for a sports franchise, cheering their heroes and deriding their foes. Nevertheless, how people remember the past is an important consideration in how they view the present and plan for the future, so it is critical to understand even flawed or incomplete perspectives as people search for an understanding of the past that serves their needs, wants, and desires.

Although people speak of the memory of the American Civil War, it is more accurate to see it as three separate yet interconnected pieces of memory. First, how did the war come about? What caused it? What were the central issues at stake, and how did they lead to secession and war? What was the role of slavery in causing the conflict? Could the crisis have been prevented? Second, why did the war turn out as it did? Why did one side win over the other? What role did resources play, and what role did battles and leaders play? Was the outcome inevitable? What role did the destruction of slavery play in the outcome? Third, why did Reconstruction turn out as it did? Was it a success, a failure, or would some other term better describe the result? Was the outcome unavoidable? What role did white attitudes towards blacks play in the process, and how did black Americans endeavor to define what freedom meant?

The questions people ask of the past and how they view it are shaped to a great extent by their interest in understanding where they are today and how they want to make sense of the world in which they live. They use their understanding of the past to establish a context for the present and at times to justify what they want to do. Thus the past is placed at the service of the present, and the result may be shaped as much by present attitudes and needs as by a desire to understand the past on its own terms. Americans' understanding of the past is often guided by the needs and wants of the present, along with their disagreements over what happened, how it happened, why it happened, and what it meant. As the historian David Blight has argued, the resulting memory that Americans have of any historical period is formed as much by what is forgotten or omitted as by what is remembered, and they may not share the same memories.

The First Generation

Until the end of the nineteenth century most accounts of the period served as little more than briefs for the perspectives of the participants. This was understandable given the role of recollection in shaping these initial narratives. Ulysses S. Grant, for example, crafted a two-volume memoir that argued for the justice of the Union cause and the central role played by debates over slavery and its future in the debates leading up to the war and in the Confederate founding. Confederate leaders such as Jefferson Davis and Alexander H. Stephens maintained the justice of the Confederate cause, which they decoupled from a defense of slavery (in contrast to their wartime positions). Rather, they claimed, it was a war over the meaning of the Constitution, specifically over states' rights and the legitimacy of secession.

As one might expect, accounts of the war by its participants often simply refought it. Confederate military narratives tended to argue two contradictory positions, as generals and political leaders alike pointed fingers at each other for making fatal decisions or emphasized how all would have turned out better had their advice been heeded, all the while insisting that in any case Union resources were so overwhelming as to leave little doubt as to who would ultimately prevail. That such a conclusion rendered irrelevant efforts to praise or blame various generals or politicians as responsible for that outcome—what difference would it make if the road to Appomattox was preordained?—did not deter them from engaging in the exercise. If it was a lost cause, it was also a gallant one, of which Confederates need not be ashamed as they defended home and hearth from an evil invader.

Union accounts of the war parceled out credit and blame from the perspective of the writer, and at times it looked as if the fiercest fighting was between the Union generals, with their battling the

Confederates a mere afterthought. These narratives avoided the question of inevitability, because to concede that the Union was destined to win from the outset would have denigrated the contributions made by the bluecoats to preserving the Union through their own exploits; that some generals and their advocates did their best to diminish the accomplishments of Grant and Sherman was largely due to their efforts to make a case for the forgotten brilliance of their predecessors or rivals. Little was said about the revolutionary impact of the war or how it destroyed slavery.

Accounts of Reconstruction reflected the same need to amplify and justify positions taken during the event itself. There was little attempt to gain dispassionate or disinterested distancing from such a recent event, although one could see in most descriptions penned by white people very little interest in how blacks attempted to shape their postwar world. At a time when segregation and Jim Crow were in the ascendant, there was little chance that accounts of Reconstruction by white Southerners would denounce anti-black violence, although accounts of corruption and malfeasances by Republicans white and black were plentiful. And while black voices recalled the horrors of terrorist bloodshed and the frustration of seeking equality and protection, they did not circulate widely; the majority of white Northerners simply wanted to move ahead with their lives and away from a past that seemed too murky and distasteful to confront directly. Wasn't preserving the Union and destroying slavery enough?

As veterans aged and the war itself drifted into the past, white Northerners proved less insistent on pressing home their victory. Given the doubts of many white Northerners about the viability of black equality, they did not mourn the failure of Reconstruction. White Southerners established a narrative extolling Southern culture, bravery, honor, female virtue, and manliness that manifested itself in a time of refinement and reflection, all made possible by the labor of well-treated, happy slaves. Despite their best efforts and through no fault of their own, they suffered defeat at the hands of the more numerous, better supplied, and well-fed

The Lost Cause *by Henry Mosler, painted in 1869, is a stark portrayal of the sense of loss felt by many ex-Confederates in the aftermath of the Civil War.*

A group of Civil War
veterans belonging to the
Grand Army of the Republic
(GAR) meet in the early
twentieth century. The GAR
played an important role in
commemorating the sacrifices
made in the war.

Yankees, who in turn found themselves on the losing end when it came to Reconstruction.

The Lost Cause Resurgent

During the first half of the twentieth century an understanding of the Civil War and Reconstruction emerged which was very comforting to many Southern whites, especially as this emerging view virtually eliminated white Southern Unionists and dissent within the Confederacy from the narrative. Most historians portrayed the coming sectional crisis as rooted in economic conflict, cultural and social differences, or contrasting views of the Constitution, while skirting around the issue of slavery, which they often portrayed as a benevolent institution that was already in decline. Some went so far as to say that what should have been an avoidable conflict exploded because of the bumbling short-sightedness of political leaders and the fanaticism of extremists, especially abolitionists. The antebellum South of romance and refinement battled against an aggressive and ambitious Yankee business culture that wanted to use government to advance its interests, as if white Southerners had never had the same idea.

Mainstream treatments of the war followed suit, extolling the leadership of Confederate generals (including the near-deification of Robert E. Lee, especially by Douglas Southall Freeman) and the bravery of Confederate soldiers in accounts that emphasized the war in the eastern theater. In contrast, most scholars presented Grant as an unimaginative mediocrity who bashed his way to victory and prevailed due to his superior resources, while William T. Sherman and Philip H. Sheridan waged a devastatingly destructive and vindictive war against civilians and property. It would be left to British military historians J. F. C. Fuller and B. H. Liddell Hart to present Grant and Sherman in a more positive light as the prophets of modern war. While scholars tended to extol Lincoln's evident superiority over Davis, they questioned his commitment to emancipation and equality, seeing the former as due to military necessity and as a way to deter European intervention. For all of the emphasis on the superiority of Confederate military leadership, most accounts still conceded that Union victory, absent a major upset, was only a matter of time.

Most Americans came to view Reconstruction as a disastrous enterprise in pursuit of a fool's errand. Scholarly studies, many undertaken under the guidance of William A. Dunning, emphasized the corruption of carpetbaggers (white Northerners), the knavery of scalawags (white Southern Republicans) and the ignorance of the freedpeople in the construction and operation of Republican state governments in the South, while other scholars lambasted congressional Republicans as vindictive and President Grant as incompetent and corrupt. Thus it was left to gallant white Southerners to save the day and restore peace to the South, in part because they knew best how to work with their former slaves. W. E. B. DuBois offered a powerful challenge to this consensus in *Black Reconstruction in America* (1935), but most people overlooked his work at the time.

The findings of scholars often fail to make their way to the minds of the general public, but this was not the case when it came to the Civil War and Reconstruction in the first half of the twentieth century. Although memorials to Lincoln and Grant dominated both ends of Washington, D.C.'s National Mall, the erection of monuments in the South to Confederate heroes proceeded apace, especially in Richmond and New Orleans. Popular colorful histories with such arresting titles as *The Tragic Era* offered a doom-and-gloom rendering of Reconstruction. Far more powerful, however, were two films based upon novels: *Birth of a Nation* (1915), in which director D. W. Griffith presented the Ku Klux Klan as rescuers of civilization and preservers of law and order against blacks unfit for freedom and their venal white allies, and *Gone with the Wind* (1939), which celebrated Confederates' courage and honor as they attempted to fend off the evil foe (even as lead character Rhett Butler voices reservations about such values), followed by the struggles of white Southerners to rebuild in the face of Yankee oppression during Reconstruction. Enslaved blacks were loyal, happy, and stayed with their former owners after emancipation. Masterpieces of cinematography, both films told gripping stories of love, lust, and violence (including sexual violence) in vivid fashion and celebrated the triumph of white supremacy as the restoration of the natural order of things. That African Americans protested against both movies was beside the point in the eyes of the appreciative audiences; indeed, *Birth of a Nation* actually portrayed Lincoln in a positive light, suggesting that his murder prevented a far easier reconciliation than was the case.

Revisionism, Reassessment, and Resistance

The advent of World War II and the ensuing civil rights movement during the Cold War struck at the heart of these interpretations. One could not fight a war to save democracy while sanctioning inequality at home; one could not proclaim a victory for freedom while honoring a cause that featured an endorsement of enslaving fellow human beings. Slowly but surely, matters of slavery and race returned to the center of the story. Although several scholars rehabilitated the reputation of the

- THE FIERY CROSS OF THE KU KLUX KLAN -

D.W.GRIFFITH'S MIGHTY SPECTACLE

THE BIRTH OF A NATION FOUNDED ON THOMAS DIXON'S 'THE CLANSMAN'

A theatrical poster for Birth of a Nation, *the infamous 1915 film which presented the Ku Klux Klan as modern crusaders destined to preserve white supremacy against an encroaching African American threat.*

abolitionists as advocates of equality, accounts of the coming of the war emphasized economic and political aspects of slavery as well as a growing Northern resistance to Southern efforts to protect the "peculiar institution." Whether the war was inevitable was now framed in terms of whether white Southerners would have ever acceded to a program that would have brought about, however gradually, the end of slavery.

Accounts of the military history of the war offered a more favorable view of Grant's generalship, especially in the writings of Bruce Catton. Descriptions of military operations gave increased recognition to campaigns west of the Appalachian Mountains and along the Mississippi River valley. Still, the notion that both sides should be honored for what they believed in died hard, and Shelby Foote's massive three-volume history of the war did what it could to downplay issues of slavery, race, and freedom. Accounts of the war eventually moved beyond battles and leaders to look at the changes wrought by the conflict as well as the roles played by women and African Americans in shaping the course and outcome of the struggle. Scholars pointed out that, while the Confederacy might have won its independence outright on the battlefield, its best chance for victory lay in undermining Northern support for the war, a goal it had come close to achieving in 1864. So much for an inevitable Union victory; the Vietnam War (1955–75) reminded Americans that the side with the most men and resources did not always prevail.

However, scholarly understanding of Reconstruction underwent a drastic change. Now Reconstruction was seen as a tragedy because it did not succeed in securing equality and opportunity for African Americans. Had there been more far-reaching changes, including the confiscation and redistribution of plantation holdings, blacks might have secured a far firmer foundation upon which to advance. Eventually scholars also understood the role of violence and intimidation in overthrowing Republican governments; they questioned whether Reconstruction was indeed radical enough, arguing that institutional and

ideological conservatism joined forces with residual white racism in the North to limit what could be done. Andrew Johnson, once a figure over whom scholars debated, began his slow slide to the bottom of presidential performance rankings, while scholars began to view Ulysses S. Grant's presidency in a more positive light, resulting in his rise through the same ranking system to the middle of the pack. Reconstruction became a moment of black achievement challenged by violent white racism.

These revised understandings slowly made their way into school textbooks and popular consciousness, resisted in large part by white Southerners who held dear to their notions of a genteel institution of enslavement, complete with loyal and happy slaves (if one admitted that one's ancestors actually owned slaves); a continued celebration of the Confederate war effort, which had little if anything to do with slavery; and resistance to the idea that Reconstruction was anything but an evil Yankee Republican plot foiled by brave white Southerners. Coming at a time when white Southerners waved Confederate flags and sang "Dixie" as they resisted the civil rights movement, the integration of schools, and the removal of barriers to voting—all achieved with some degree of federal intervention—the need to defend the past in the present seemed all too clear. Confederate general Nathan Bedford Forrest, long reputed to be the leader of the Reconstruction Klan, became a celebrated hero, while work was completed on a tremendous monument to Confederate leadership on the slopes of Stone Mountain, Georgia, where twentieth-century reiterations of the Reconstruction Klan appeared. But white Southerners were not the only ones reluctant to abandon the notion that the Civil War was little more than a dispute between brothers: to many people interested in the Civil War, both sides fought for what they believed in, and that was

good enough as they studied the movements of armies and the clash of arms at many a battlefield. Such was the case at the celebrations of the war's centennial between 1961 and 1965; although commemorations some 25 years later were more subdued, it remained a contest where both sides could claim honor.

Memory, Reckoning, and Removal

As the twenty-first century approached, historians became more aware of the role of memory in shaping popular understandings of history and examined the ways in which Americans engaged in forming their memories of the past with present concerns in mind or to serve various agendas. Few

The creation of the massive memorial of Confederate leaders at Stone Mountain, Georgia, signified the continued importance of the memory of the Civil War in Southern identity.

scholars disagreed with the argument that slavery was, as Lincoln put it, "somehow" the cause of the conflict, focusing on defining and describing that "somehow." Studies of the war itself branched out beyond the traditional emphasis on battles and leaders to look even more closely at the experience of the common soldier, at the role of civilians, including women, in a nation at war, and at the destruction of slavery. Studies of Reconstruction looked at the role of violence in subverting black freedom and the ways in which institutional and ideological conservatism limited what could be done, adding the realization that the rapid restoration of civil rule placed great pressure on creating sustainable regimes that could resist violent opposition and internal friction. Once objects, black Americans were now recognized as agents working to shape their own destiny as well as that of the nation itself.

A dwindling but still significant number of white Americans, mostly from the South, resisted these findings. Proclaiming that their brandishing of Confederate battle flags was a sign of "heritage, not hate," these advocates of Southern pride equated some four centuries of history with four years of war in framing their identity as well as that of the South. However, evidence that these heritage groups interacted with white nationalist and white supremacist groups as well as a defiant Southern nationalism that continued to cling to the Confederacy as something to be studied and celebrated suggested that something else was at work here, and those implications became more apparent after the election of an African American, Barack Obama, as president in 2008 and his taking office weeks before the bicentennial of Lincoln's birth, a coincidence which gave rise to comparisons between the two men, both elected from Illinois.

The advent of the Civil War sesquicentennial two years later demonstrated that rival understandings of the Civil War continued to exist, even if many Americans placed less importance on them than was once the case. Some beliefs died hard, although the enthusiasm for commemoration at Gettysburg declined after its sesquicentennial in 2013. In 2015, just over two months after a ceremony at Appomattox Court House marked the end of most events commemorating the Civil War, the slaughter of nine African Americans in a Charleston, South Carolina, church by a gun-toting white supremacist who was fond of the Confederate flag ignited widespread controversy about Confederate symbols in racist contexts. That the massacre had taken place inside the Emanuel African Methodist Episcopal Church, which counted among its founders Denmark Vesey, a free black who was later executed for his efforts to ignite a slave insurrection in 1822, added to the context; the murderer's use of Confederate symbols led many South Carolinians to work to remove the Confederate flag still flying on the grounds of the state capitol at Columbia. That Confederate flag had flown above the dome of the state capitol between 1961 and 2000, becoming a cause of great controversy, as people increasingly linked it with white supremacy and resistance to civil rights. Now it was removed from the state grounds altogether. Elsewhere governors moved to eliminate Confederate flag-themed license plates and ceased issuing proclamations declaring April Confederate History Month.

Confederate heritage groups protested against such actions, sometimes responding by erecting their own flagpoles on private property, especially in Virginia. Before long Confederate flags were removed from Robert E. Lee's crypt at Washington and Lee Chapel in Lexington, Virginia, where traditional Lee-Jackson celebrations had become a thing of the past, despite the efforts of Confederate heritage groups to remain visible and draw attention to their cause. Once more they found allies in the ranks of white nationalist and white supremacist groups. When authorities in Charlottesville, Virginia, decided to seek the removal of two equestrian statues of Lee and Stonewall Jackson, protestors targeted Charlottesville as a place to make their stand. They pointed to the decision of New Orleans authorities, led by Mayor Mitch Landrieu, to remove three Civil War and one Reconstruction monument, as evidence that white heritage in its Confederate manifestation was under attack. The Charlottesville rally, dominated by white

nationalists and supremacists, turned violent, with one protestor using his car to run down and kill a counter-protestor. President Donald Trump's observation that there were "very fine people on both sides" inflamed the situation still further. Days after the Charlottesville protest, Baltimore carried out its decision to remove an equestrian statue of Lee and Jackson together, along with one of Chief Justice Roger B. Taney, author of an infamous majority opinion in *Dred Scott v. Sandford* (1857) that denied citizenship rights to black people.

Across the South, there were continued debates about Confederate statues and iconography. These reached a climax in 2020, when, in the aftermath of the killing of an African American, George Floyd, by a white policeman in Minneapolis, Minnesota, a wave of protests reignited debates over Confederate symbols and statues. Within weeks the portraits of four speakers of the US House of Representatives with ties to the Confederacy were taken down amid calls for the removal of several Confederate statues in the Capitol. Mississippi decided to remove the Confederate battle flag from its state flag, reversing course, while debate renewed over whether to rename United States military installations named after Confederate generals.

Such events reveal that how Americans remember the Civil War and how they draw connections between those memories and present-day political debates remains an ever-present concern. However superficial, flawed, or incomplete these understandings might be, opponents of Confederate monuments remind us that such monuments were erected as celebrations of white supremacy as well as Confederate heroism, and that Americans might rethink the practice of honoring men who betrayed oaths of loyalty and battled United States military forces in an effort to establish a new nation-state specifically dedicated to the preservation and promotion of slavery. While its commemoration has often proved divisive, the Civil War was a defining moment in the history of the United States, and it established the foundations of modern American society, with all its strengths and flaws.

The statue of Robert E. Lee in Richmond, Virginia, was erected in 1890. The statue has been the subject of intense controversy. When the governor announced its removal after the George Floyd protests of 2020, several residents filed a lawsuit to keep it aloft.

INDEX

Adams, Henry 171
Adams, John Quincy 20
Allen, E.J. 70
Anthony, Susan B. 114
Antietam, Battle of 79, 80–1

Babcock, Orville E. 176
Banks, Nathaniel 90, 107, 122–3
Barnard, George N. 113
Beauregard, G. T. 42, 43, 44, 55, 57, 126
Bell, John 30
Birth of a Nation 183, 184
Black Reconstruction in America (DuBois) 183
Blair, Francis P. 140
Booth, John Wilkes 152
Brady, Matthew 113
Bragg, Braxton 83, 100–1
Breckinridge, John C. 30
Brooks, Preston 25
Brown, John 28–9
Brown, Joseph E. 112, 137
Brownlow, William G. 157
Buchanan, James 25
Buell, Don Carlos 55, 56, 83
Bull Run, First Battle of 42–5
Bull Run, Second Battle of 77–9
Burnside, Ambrose 80, 83, 85, 91–2, 101, 123
Butler, Andrew 25
Butler, Benjamin F. 39, 107, 122, 125–6

Calhoun, John C. 19, 20, 22
Catton, Bruce 185
Chancellorsville, Battle of 91–3
Chattanooga campaign 100–1
Chase, Samuel P. 25, 139
Clay, Henry 17, 18, 20, 22, 23, 72
Cleburne, Patrick 140
Colfax, Schuyler 173
Colfax massacre 173–4, 175
Corinth, Battle of 82, 83
Crater, Battle of the 127, 129
Crittenden, John J. 39
Cuffee, Paul 18
Curtis, Samuel R. 65
Constitutional Convention 13, 14

Davis, David 177
Davis, Jefferson
    as provisional President of Confederate
        States of America 32
    and First Battle of Bull Run 43
    as President of Confederacy 58
    and Robert E. Lee 62
    and Battle of Gettysburg 94
    and Chattanooga campaign 100
    deals with dissent 112
    and 1864 campaign 129, 130
    in final stage of Civil War 140
    recollections of 180
Douglas, Stephen A. 22, 24, 28, 158
Douglass, Frederick 116
DuBois, W. E. B. 183
Dunning, William A. 183

Early, Jubal 127, 128, 129, 132
Ewell, Richard S. 94, 95

Farragut, David G. 131, 158
Five Forks, Battle of 143, 144–5
Floyd, George 188
Foote, Andrew H. 53
Foote, Shelby 185
Forrest, Nathan Bedford 186
Fredericksburg, Battle of 85–7
Freeman, Douglas Southall 183
Frémont, John Charles 25, 40, 47–8, 53, 73
Fuller, J. F. C. 183

Gardner, Alexander 113
Garfield, James A. 173
Garrison, William Lloyd 18–19
Gettysburg, Battle of 94–9
Godkin, Edwin L. 171
Gone with the Wind 183
Grant, Ulysses S.
    on causes of Civil War 11
    securing border states 47
    emergence of 53–5, 102
    and Battle of Shiloh 55, 56–7
    and escalation of Civil War 68
    at Iuka 83
    siege of Vicksburg 87, 89–91, 99, 113

and Chattanooga campaign 101
recruitment problems 108
and prisoner exchange 109
civilian view of 113
and African American recruitment 116
and 1864 campaign 119, 121–30, 132
in final stage of Civil War 137, 141–2, 143,
    146, 147
and Reconstruction 155, 159, 160
in 1868 Presidential campaign 160, 164, 167
Reconstruction as President 167–77
recollections of 180
public perception after Civil War 183, 185
Greeley, Horace 75–6, 130, 171, 172–3
Grierson, Benjamin 90
Griffiths, D.W. 183

Halleck, Henry 53, 55, 56, 57, 121
Hampton, Wade 142
Hancock, Winfield S. 97
Hayes, Rutherford B. 160, 175
Hill, A.P. 94, 97
Hood, John Bell 113, 129, 132, 137, 138
Hooker, Joseph 91–3, 95
Hunter, David 73, 74

Jackson, Andrew 18, 19, 20
Jackson, Thomas J. "Stonewall"
    and First Battle of Bull Run 43
    and defence of Washington 60, 62
    and Battle of Chancellorsville 92
    public perception of after Civil War 188
Jefferson, Thomas 13
Johnson, Andrew 39, 55, 87, 130, 139, 153–9,
    163, 165, 185
Johnson, Reverdy 74
Johnston, Albert Sydney 55, 56–7, 62, 129, 143
Johnston, Joseph E. 42, 43, 143, 146–7

Kenner, Duncan 140
Kernstown, Battle of 60
Key, David M. 177

Landrieu, Mitch 188
Lee, Robert E. 102
    start of Civil War 35

PICTURE CREDITS

t = top, b = bottom, l = left, r = right

Alamy: 14, 23, 24, 65b, 107, 113t, 146, 161, 163, 171, 176

Bridgeman Images: 51

Boston Public Library: 16

David Woodroffe: 63b

Flickr: 156 (Architect of the Capitol/Allyn Cox)

Getty Images: 12b, 27, 31, 38, 64, 129t, 131t, 135, 138b

Library of Congress: 10, 22, 25, 29, 32, 33, 34, 35, 36, 41, 43, 44, 46, 49, 52, 54b, 55, 57, 59, 60, 61, 62l, 62r, 63t, 68, 71, 72, 73, 74, 75, 76, 77, 78, 81, 82, 83, 85, 86, 88, 91, 92, 93, 94, 96, 100tl, 100tr, 100b, 101, 102, 104, 106, 108t, 110, 111t, 111b, 112, 116, 117, 118, 119, 120, 121, 122t, 122b, 123, 126t, 127, 128t, 128b, 130, 132t, 132b, 133t, 133b, 134, 136, 137, 138t, 139, 140, 141b, 144, 148, 150b, 151, 153, 154, 158, 162, 164, 165, 168, 169t, 169b, 170, 173, 174b, 175, 177, 182

Library of Virginia: 18

Metropolitan Museum of Art: 70, 98

National Archives and Records Administration, USA: 45, 54t, 56, 109, 159, 166

New York Public Library: 13, 19, 21, 40, 84

Shutterstock: 178, 186, 187, 189

Smithsonian Institute: 65t (National Museum of African American History and Culture), 124 (American Art Museum), 152 (National Museum of American History)

Wikimedia Commons: 12t, 15, 17, 20, 26, 28, 37, 42, 48, , 66, 69, 90, 97, 103, 108b, 113b, 114t, 114b, 125, 126b, 129b, 131b, 141t, 142, 147, 150t, 157, 172, 174t, 181, 184, 185